The Complete Book of Rules

TIME-TESTED SECRETS
FOR CAPTURING THE HEART
OF MR RIGHT

Ellen Fein and Sherrie Schneider

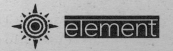

Element
An Imprint of HarperCollins*Publishers*
77–85 Fulham Palace Road,
Hammersmith, London W6 8JB

The website address is: www.thorsonselement.com

◉ element ™

and *Element* are trademarks of
HarperCollins*Publishers* Ltd

First published individually as *The Rules* (1995)
and *The Rules II* (1997)

Revised edition published by Thorsons,
an Imprint of HarperCollins*Publishers* 2000
This edition published by Element 2003

14

© Ellen Fein and Sherrie Schneider 2000

Ellen Fein and Sherrie Schneider assert the moral
right to be identified as the authors of this work

A catalogue record for this book is available
from the British Library

ISBN 0 7225 3974 6

Printed and bound in Great Britain by
Clays Ltd, St Ives plc

Contents

Introduction

The Rules Phenomenon

Seven years ago, when we set out to write *The Rules*, we knew that we had an important message to share. We believed in *The Rules*. We had seen them work time and time again in our own lives, in our close circle of girlfriends and an ever-widening circle of friends and acquaintances, as well as co-workers and relatives.

When our phones began ringing off the hook with dating questions and (eventually) success stories, we knew we had to write *The Rules* in book form to make it available to *all* women.

Lo and behold, *The Rules* became not just a bestselling book, but a phenomenon, revolutionizing dating practices around the world.

In fact, *The Rules* became so popular that it achieved a kind of pop culture status. It was spoofed on *Saturday Night Live* ('Get the ring!'), used as the plot for several TV sitcoms and also inspired a number of parody books including *Breaking the Rules* ('Stare straight at men and talk incessantly') and *Rules for Cats* ('Don't accept a trip to the vet after Wednesday').

Suddenly, *The Rules* was everywhere! A financial publication ran an article on the rules for investing ('Don't buy on Friday if your broker calls after Wednesday') and a political columnist wrote that one presidential candidate might have won the election if he had just tried to be a 'creature unlike any other'.

Why all the fuss? Why all the interest in *The Rules* when there are dozens of other dating books on the market? Why has *The Rules* become such a phenomenon?

The answer is simple: *The Rules* work! Unlike other dating books that are therapeutic and theoretical – that sound good, that give warm n fuzzy, meaningless and misleading advice such as *be yourself, don't play games, tell a man how you feel,* but don't work in real life – *The Rules* tells the truth about dating and helps you get Mr Right!

The Rules take the analysis and angst out of dating. It's simple. If he calls you, he likes you. If he doesn't, *Next!* What does *be yourself* mean if that's calling a man three times a day or staying on the phone for three hours? Why would anyone want to read a dating book that didn't help you get the man you want to marry you?

Many people ask how we wrote a best-seller. To be honest, we were not trying to. We wrote *The Rules* to help women date with self-esteem and get married. Period.

While we are naturally thrilled by the success of the book, what's been even more rewarding is seeing how women of all ages and all walks of life use *The Rules* to love themselves and marry Mr Right. After three decades of haphazard dating – Dutch treat, sex on the first date and living together – these women are delighted that such a dating book exists.

'I wish I had known about *The Rules* ten years ago,' is the most frequent comment we hear.

'*The Rules* should be given out to all women at birth,' wrote another *Rules* fan.

The book hit a chord not only with single women in their twenties, thirties and forties, but with mothers and grandmothers. 'She won't listen to me, maybe she'll listen to you,' wrote one mum. Another mum told us she gave the book to her daughter and her daughter's friends.

While many readers thanked us for the general guidelines provided in *The Rules*, just as many wrote and called asking for more specific answers to dating situations and problems – for example, rules for long-distance relationships, rules for getting back an ex-boyfriend, rules for dating a celebrity, rules for dating a co-worker, rules for turning a male friend into a boyfriend, rules for dating services and on-line dating, among many other topics.

So in 1997 we wrote *The Rules II* to answer all these questions – and to clarify any confusion you might have about rules in the first book, such as, 'How will he know the real me if I do *The Rules*?' and 'Can I *ever* call a man?'

Of course, as popular as *The Rules* have become, it has also been the subject of controversy – mostly by the media and the authors of other dating books, not by women who simply want advice about men. They just want to get married!

The Rules have been criticized for being old-fashioned and antifeminist, and for encouraging women to play games and get married at any cost ('get the ring'). We would like to examine these criticisms one by one and explain why they are unfounded.

Old fashioned? Not really. While *The Rules* may sound like something your mother may have told you about, times and circumstances have completely changed. Women today need *The Rules* – not because pursuing men is morally wrong or scandalous, or for any of the reasons your mother may have told you. No, *The Rules* tell us not to pursue men for one simple reason. It doesn't work.

Fifty years ago, women didn't call men or live with men before marriage because it was considered socially unacceptable. Fifty years ago, they didn't even need to think about 'ending the date first'. Their fathers ended it for them by requiring them to be home at a certain time, much like their great-grandfathers put an end to dates by holding up a shotgun on the front porch!

In addition, back then, women often had to get married in order to move out of their parents' home. Women were financially dependent on men and once married they became full-time wives and mothers who, for the most part, did not pursue careers.

Compare that to women today. Many are financially self-sufficient. They can afford their own homes, cars, holidays, wardrobes and creature comforts. They can even have or adopt and support a child on their own. They no longer need men to get away from their parents or to lead good or interesting lives. But the truth is they want men in their lives – as partners/ friends, lovers, husbands/fathers. They can function without men, but they yearn for marriage and children and/or fulfilling relationships.

Who or what can women turn to for dating advice? They may or may not be able to relate to their mothers. Besides, some mothers, trying to be hip and modern or desperate for their daughters to get married and produce a grandchild, will give them bad advice and tell them to call men and pay their own way. ('Don't be so picky,' they tell them.)

Their female friends, conditioned by the social mores of today and with well-meaning intentions, may say 'Oh, call him if you like him! What have you got to lose?' If he turns them down, 'So, what?' they say.

Well we say:

1 Maybe if you don't call him, he'll build up a real desire and call you!

2 A man who is receptive to your advances (without making any of his own) may date or even marry you at your suggestion, but down the road he'll be bored and ambivalent toward you.

Women have turned to *The Rules* because it's the only advice they can count on that works. They're not retro, they're fabulous!

Antifeminist? No, as far as we are concerned, there is no conflict between *The Rules* and feminism. *Rules* girls can be feminists. We are feminists. We believe in and are grateful for the advances women have made in the last century. How else could we have become authors and formed a company? All women have different definitions of feminism, but to us, it is about getting equal pay for equal work. It's about women being authors, astronauts, doctors, lawyers, CEOs or whatever they want to be – getting promoted, being treated the same and paid as much as men!

Feminism is also about women believing in their own importance. It is about being fulfilled by our jobs, our hobbies, our friendships. It is knowing that the women in our lives are as important as the men – and treating our friends with respect and consideration to prove it!

But with all due respect, feminism has not changed men or the nature of romantic relationships. Like it or not, men are emotionally and romantically different from women. Men are biologically the aggressor. They thrive on challenge – whether it's the stock market, basketball or football – while women crave security and bonding. This has been true since civilization began!

Men who respond to *The Rules* are not sick or stupid, but quite normal and healthy. Your average guy. What would be sick is if a man chased and chased a woman who clearly didn't want him, who repeatedly said 'no' when he asked her out as early as Monday for Saturday night. But that's not what we're talking about. We're talking about a woman who says 'yes' to dates when asked a few days in advance and is nice to men on dates.

She's simply not too eager and doesn't drop everything to see him at a moment's notice. That way he respects her and wants to be with her and marry her.

Why men are naturally driven by challenge is not important. The point is to do what works to have a successful relationship, which is to let men do the pursuing ... in other words, to follow *The Rules*.

After twenty or thirty years of do-what-you-feel and haphazard dating, most women we know are actually relieved to have rules and boundaries to live by. These women are happy that feminism has helped them get ahead in business and given them financial independence, but they agree that trying to be as aggressive in relationships with men as they are in their careers doesn't work.

Are we telling women to play games? Some people like to focus on the most superficial aspects in *The Rules* – the ones most likely to promote controversy – but the book is really about self-esteem, about setting boundaries. Yes, in some ways, you're playing a game. The game is called liking yourself! The game is not accepting just any treatment from a man. The game is being true to your heart. Everyone knows in their hearts that *The Rules* work, that this is the way it really is. But some people have to read the book a few times before they get the message that it's not just about egg timers, lipstick and not returning calls.

The Rules is not an etiquette book – it's not about how to order wine on a date or which fork to use. While these niceties are important, they're not what *The Rules* focus on. *The Rules* are about saving women – and men, for that matter – heartache. There are many disastrous relationships out there because women either initiated relationships with men or kept them going long after they should have been over. A failed relationship is depressing, confidence-shaking and altogether unpleasant. By following *The Rules*, you avoid these disastrous results – and these painful emotions.

We had to write *The Rules* strictly, like a strict diet book, because we knew women would break them. They always sneak in their favourite high-fat meal or a piece of chocolate cake on Saturday nights. With such strict rules, even if women break the occasional rule, they can still reap the benefits of doing the rest.

Even therapists, whom we were sure would find the 'be mysterious' part of *The Rules* objectionable, are actually recommending the book to their clients. They agree that the openness and honesty so necessary in therapy do not work in the initial stages of dating.

Are *The Rules* too marriage-minded? No, just realistic. Many women want to get married, and why not? It's great to have a wonderful man to share your life with – end of story. We're not telling women they're nothing without a man. It's just that many women feel that if they don't marry a nice guy, they're missing something. It's a fact. This is how they really feel. It's not a moral issue. Can they be happy without a husband? Sure. Can you be happy without taking holidays? Sure, but why would you want to?

We are not advocating marriage at any cost. On the contrary, in *Rule 42*: *'Buyer Beware'*, we explain how to determine if he's *Mr Right*. This is a thinking woman's guide to marriage. This is not about being a Stepford wife.

Indeed, *The Rules* represents a change in attitude about dating, a new spirituality that is sorely needed today. It's going against nature when you chase a man, sleep with him too soon or beg him to marry you. He may end up mistreating you, even if he marries you. He may never forgive you for trapping him and treat you badly.

Conversely, when you do *The Rules* on a man who initially showed interest, he gets to fall in love with you and value you. He does not take you for granted. Every phone call and date is precious. He never feels trapped or that you pressured him to marry you because he did the calling, the pursuing, the proposing.

Rules marriages are happy marriages. *Rules* husbands make wonderful partners for life. They are attentive and involved husbands and fathers. They change diapers, help the kids with their homework and plan family holidays.

The Rules work. They really do. That's why women who want to be happily married – or at the very least, in a loving relationship – are living by *The Rules* – and loving the results.

1 | The History of *The Rules*

No one seems to remember exactly how *The Rules* got started, but we think they began circa 1917 with Melanie's grandmother who made men wait nervously in her parents' front room in a small suburb of Michigan. Back then, they called it 'playing hard to get'. Whatever you call it, she had more marriage proposals than shoes. Grandma passed on her know-how to Melanie's mother, who passed it on to Melanie. It had been a family treasure for nearly a century. But when Melanie got married in 1981, she freely offered this old-fashioned advice to her single college friends and co-workers, like us.

At first, Melanie whispered *The Rules*. After all, modern women aren't to talk loudly about wanting to get married. We had grown up dreaming about being the president of a company, not the wife of the president. So, we quietly passed *The Rules* on from friend to friend, somewhat embarrassed because they seemed so, well, 50s. Still, we had to face it: as much as we loved being powerful in business, for most of us, that just wasn't enough. Like our mothers and grandmothers before us, we also wanted husbands who would be our best friends. Deep inside, if the truth be told, we really wanted to get married – the romance, the gown, the flowers, the presents, the honeymoon – the whole package. We didn't want to give up our liberation, but neither did we want to come home to empty flats. Who said we couldn't have it all?

If you think *The Rules* are crazy, don't worry, so did we. But after much heartache we came to believe that *The Rules* aren't immoral or outlandish, just a simple working set of behaviours and reactions that, when followed, invariably serve to make most women irresistible to desirable men. Why not admit it? We needed *The Rules*! Women today simply have not been schooled in the basics – *The Rules* of finding a husband or at least being very popular with men.

Soon, we got bolder and began to talk louder. These *Rules* – they worked!

At first, we were uncomfortable with some of the premises which seemed to fly in the face of everything we'd been taught about male–female relations; but – there was no getting around it – success talked. We swallowed some of our preconceived theories, followed *The Rules* faithfully and watched as so many of us got married (along with being career women or whatever else we were).

There we were – a secret underground, sharing the magic, passing it on, doing what historically women have done for each other since the world began –

networking for success. This time, though, the stakes were larger and the victories sweeter than any corporate deal. We're talking marriage here – real, lasting marriage, not just loveless mergers – the result of doing *The Rules*. The simple *Rules*. The How-to-Find-a-Great-Husband *Rules*.

For years, we had been sharing them with the women we knew, both at home and at work. For years, women had been calling us to check up on points: 'Did you say that you have to end the date first or he does? I forget.'

Then one night, during a Chinese dinner with a few of our single friends, we heard Cindy mention something about these ... er, *Rules* ... that she'd heard about from a friend in California. We knew it! There could be no mistake. These were the same *Rules* one of us had followed in New York to find her wonderful husband. *The Rules* had criss-crossed the country, bouncing from woman to woman, from suburb to city, until here they came right back to us over egg rolls in Manhattan!

But – and here's the catch – Cindy got them wrong!

'*The Rule* says men have to end the date first so that they're in charge,' said Cindy.

'No, no, no, WRONG. *The Rule* is you end the date first so that you leave him wanting you more,' we explained.

It was then that we decided to write *The Rules* down so that there would be no mistakes.

2 | What are *The Rules*?

How many times have you heard someone say, 'She's nice, she's pretty, she's smart ... why isn't she married?' Were they talking about you, perhaps? Ever wonder why women who are not so pretty or smart attract men almost effortlessly?

Frankly, many women we know find it easier to relocate to another city, switch careers or run a marathon than get the right man to marry them! If this sounds like you, then you need *The Rules*!

What are *The Rules*? They are a simple way of acting around men that can help any woman win the heart of the man of her dreams. Sound too good to be true? We were sceptical at first, too. Read on!

The purpose of *The Rules* is to make Mr Right obsessed with having you as his by making yourself seem unattainable. In plain language, we're talking about playing hard to get! Follow *The Rules*, and he will not just marry you, but feel crazy about you, forever! What we're promising you is 'happily ever after'. A marriage truly made in heaven.

If you follow *The Rules*, you can rest assured that your husband will treat you like a queen – even when he's angry with you. Why? Because he spent so much time trying to get you. You have become so precious to him that he doesn't take you for granted. On the contrary, he thinks of you constantly. He's your best friend, your Rock of Gibraltar during bad times. He's hurt if you *don't* share your problems with him. He is always there for you – when you start your new job, if you need surgery. He even likes to get involved in mundane things, such as picking out a new bedspread. He always wants to do things *together*.

When you do *The Rules*, you don't have to worry about him chasing other women, even your very attractive neighbour or his bosomy secretary. That's because when you do *The Rules*, he somehow thinks you're the sexiest woman alive! When you do *The Rules*, you don't have to worry about being abandoned, neglected or ignored!

A woman we know who followed *The Rules* is now married to a wonderful man who doesn't try to get rid of her to go out with the guys. Instead, he becomes slightly jealous when she does her own thing. They are very good friends, too.

Men are different from women. Women who call men, ask them out, conveniently have two tickets to a show or offer sex on the first date destroy male ambition and animal drive. Men are born to respond to challenge. Take away challenge and their interest wanes. That, in a nutshell, is the premise of *The Rules*. Sure, a man might marry you if you don't do *The Rules*, but we can't guarantee that yours will be a good marriage.

This is how it works: if men love challenge, we become challenging! But don't ask a man if he loves challenge. He may think or even say he doesn't. He may not realize how he reacts. *Pay attention to what he does, not what he says.*

As you read this book, you may think that *The Rules* are too calculating and wonder, 'How hard to get do I have to be? Am I never to cook him dinner or take him to the theatre? What if I just feel like talking to him? Can't I call? When may I reveal personal things about myself?'

The answer is: Read *The Rules*. Follow them completely (not a la carte) and you will be happy you did. How many of us know women who never quite trust their husbands and always feel slightly insecure? They may even see therapists to talk about why their husbands don't pay attention to them. *The Rules* will save you about fifty pounds an hour in therapy bills.

Of course, it's easy to do *The Rules* with men you're not that interested in. Naturally, you don't call them, instantly return their calls or send them love letters. Sometimes your indifference makes them so crazy about you that you end up marrying one of them. That's because you did *The Rules* (without even thinking about it) and he proposed!

But settling for less is not what this book is about. The idea is to do *The Rules* with the man you're really crazy about. This will require effort, patience and self-restraint. But isn't it worth it? Why should you compromise and marry someone who loves you but whom you're not crazy about? We know many women who face this dilemma. But don't worry – this book will help you marry only Mr Right!

Your job now is to treat the man you are really, really crazy about like the man you're not that interested in – don't call, be busy sometimes! Do all of this from the beginning – from day one! Do it from the second you meet him – or should we say, the second he meets you! The better you do *The Rules* from the beginning, the harder he will fall for you.

Keep thinking, 'How would I behave if I weren't that interested in him?' And then behave that way. Would you offer endless encouragement to someone you didn't really like? Would you stay on the phone with him for hours? Of course not!

Don't worry that busyness and lack of interest will drive him away. The men you don't like keep calling after you've turned them down, don't they?

Remember, *The Rules* are not about getting just any man to adore you and propose; they're about getting the man of your dreams to marry you! It's an old-fashioned formula, but it really works!

We understand why modern, career-oriented women have sometimes scoffed at our suggestions. They've been MBA-trained to 'make things happen' and to take charge of their careers. However, a relationship with a man is different from a job. In a relationship, the man must take charge. He must propose. We are not making this up – biologically, he's the aggressor.

Some women complain that *The Rules* prevent them from being themselves or having fun. 'Why should dating be work?' some ask. But when they end up alone on Saturday night because they did not follow *The Rules*, they always come back to us saying, 'Okay, okay, tell me what to do.'

Doing what you want to do is not always in your best interest. On a job interview, you don't act 'like yourself'. You don't eat cake if you're serious about losing weight. Similarly, it is not wise to let it all hang out and break *The Rules* as soon as you begin dating a man.

In the long run, it's not fun to break *The Rules*! You could easily end up alone. Think long-term. Imagine a husband you love, beautiful sex, children, companionship and growing old with someone who thinks you're a great catch.

Think about never having to be alone on Saturday nights or having to ask your married friends to fix you up. Think about being a couple! Unfortunately, however, you must experience some delayed gratification in the first few months of the relationship to achieve this marital bliss. But has wearing your heart on your sleeve ever got you anywhere?

There are many books and theories on this subject. All make wonderful promises, but *The Rules* actually produce results. It's easy to know what's going on when you do *The Rules*. It's very simple. If he calls you, pursues you, asks you out, it's *The Rules*. If you have to make excuses for his behaviour – for example, he didn't call after the first date because he's still hung up on his ex-girlfriend – and you have to think about every word he said until your head hurts and you call him, it's not *The Rules*. Forget what he's going through – for example, 'fear of commitment' or 'not ready for a relationship'. Remember, we don't play therapist when we do *The Rules*. If he calls and asks you out, it's *The Rules*. Anything else is conversation.

3 | Meet a *Rules* Girl

If you had ever met Melanie, you wouldn't have thought she was extraordinarily pretty or smart or special, but you might have noticed that she had a way of behaving around men that put prom queens to shame. Melanie did the best with what she had: she wore makeup and clothes well and acted elusive. Unlike other, prettier girls who ran after men or made themselves available every time a man called, Melanie acted indifferent – sometimes aloof, sometimes nice, but always *happy and busy*. She didn't return their calls, didn't stare at them (a dead giveaway of interest, see *Rule 3*) and always ended phone conversations first. 'I've got a million things to do' was her favourite closing line. Melanie's boyfriend eventually proposed to the one girl he thought he would never get – her!

Who hasn't met a Melanie? Haven't we all known women who seemed to be experts around men? Men don't appear to unnerve these women or trip them up. They have a certain self-confidence around men that has nothing to do with their looks or their jobs.

Melanies simply feel *good* about themselves – they can take or leave men – which makes men *have* to have them. Call it reverse psychology or whatever you want, but Melanies always get their man.

When you meet a Melanie, especially a plain and simple Melanie, you want to go up to her and ask, 'What is it, what are you doing that make men run after you? What's your secret? What am I doing wrong?' A genuine Melanie would probably say without too much thought, 'Oh, it's really nothing.' The born-again Melanies – former *Rules* breakers who have learned their lesson after being burned by chasing men – would probably say, 'Yes, there is a secret. Men love a challenge. Don't talk to them first, be busy sometimes, turn them down once in a while (nicely!).'

You will find Melanies everywhere you go. Watch them carefully. Observe how they have made self-contentment and independence an art form. They don't look wildly around to catch men's eyes. They don't say hello first. They just go about their business.

It would probably be good practice the next time you are at a social event to stand back and watch the Melanies and *The Rules* breakers. Compare how the two types of women behave around men and notice the results. Notice how the Melanies intentionally don't carry a pen with them in order to give men their phone numbers and they don't rush to give their business cards. Notice the way they move around the room while *The Rules* breakers stand too long in one place, look anxious or talk too long to one man. They make it

11

too easy for men to ask them out – and, as you will read in this book, that's a big mistake.

One day, after years of watching girls like Melanie snag the men of our dreams, we asked Melanie how she got such a great catch. She took pity on us and told us about *The Rules*. She said that we were nice but we talked too much and were over eager, and that we mistakenly tried to be 'friends' with men rather than elusive butterflies, or, as she put it, 'creatures unlike any other' (see *Rule 1*).

Needless to say, we were offended by what seemed to us to be downright trickery and manipulation. *The Rules* would send women back twenty-five years. What would the feminists say? On the other hand, Melanie had what we wanted: the husband of her dreams who adored her. It made sense to rethink our offended psyches!

Melanie assured us that plain-looking women who followed *The Rules* stood a better chance of being happily married than gorgeous women who didn't. Thinking back on our own dating history, it did appear that the men we really wanted didn't necessarily want us. We'd be ourselves, friendly and supportive and they thought we were great – but it ended right there. And, come to think of it, the ones we didn't particularly care for, the ones we didn't notice, maybe even snubbed, were the ones who didn't stop calling, the ones who were crazy about us. There was a message here somewhere: treat the men we wanted like the men we didn't want.

Simple, but not easy. But what did we have to lose? We wanted what Melanie had. So we did what she did, and – it worked!

4 | But First the Product – You!

Before *The Rules* can be applied for the best, most unbelievable results – the man of your dreams asking you to marry him – you have to be the best you can be. Certainly not perfect or gorgeous, but the best you can be, so …

Look your best! The better you look, the better you will feel and the more desirable you will become to him. Maybe other men will start finding you more attractive and asking you out. You will no longer feel that the man you're currently dating is the only man on earth. You'll be less anxious and more confident. And when you look and feel good, you're less likely to break *The Rules*.

We are not nutritionists, but we do know that eating right – protein, fruits and vegetables – makes you feel good. And that exercise releases endorphins which make you feel happier and more energetic. So, in addition to a healthy diet, we strongly suggest that you shake your buns! Join a gym, buy an exercise video or go jogging in a nearby park (also a great place to meet men who are jogging or walking their dogs). Make exercise exciting by playing music while you do sit-ups.

Diet and exercise and *The Rules* have a lot in common. Both require putting long-term goals before short-term gratification. You will have to experience a certain amount of discomfort when you can't eat a cream bun and you can't call a man. But you want to be fit and you want to get married so you do what you have to do. Make friends with a woman in the same predicament and jog together, go to dances together and reprimand each other when either of you is tempted to break *The Rules*. You don't have to do all this hard work alone!

If you are serious about finding a husband, then you must change your definition of gratification. Gratification is a man calling you, pursuing you and asking you to marry him. Gratification is not a hot fudge sundae or a hot date where you break *The Rules*!

Self-improvement will help you catch and keep a man. So try to change bad habits like slovenliness if you expect to live with a man. Men like women who are neat and clean. They also make better mothers of their children – the kind who don't lose their kids at the beach.

Now a word about clothes. If you walk around in any old clothes on the theory that what counts is only what's inside, not your outside, think again! Men like women who wear fashionable, sexy clothes in bright colours. Why not please them?

If you don't know a lot about clothes, read fashion magazines like *Cosmopolitan* and *Vogue* and books on the subject; consult a friend whose taste you admire; or enlist the help of a personal shopper at a department store. Trying on clothes by yourself in a dressing room can be overwhelming and confusing – not to mention painful if you are out of shape – so it's always good to get a second opinion. Why not a professional one? Personal shoppers can help you find clothes that look good on you and that hide your flaws, as opposed to clothes that are perhaps trendy but not flattering.

Always remember when you are shopping that you are unique, a creature unlike any other, a woman. Don't aspire to the unisex look. Buy feminine-looking clothes to wear on the weekends as well as during the work-week. Remember that you're dressing for men, not other women, so always strive to look feminine.

While it's good to keep up with the times, don't be a fashion slave. Don't spend a month's salary, say, on bell bottoms and clogs just because they happen to be in vogue this year. First of all, they may not be around next season, and, more importantly, you may not look good in them! We know women who have gone overboard with one look – be it man-tailored suits or oversized crocheted sweaters – and ended up looking overdressed, trendy and not at all sexy. Be a smart shopper, not a runaway spender! Buy a few good classics and mix them with cheaper items.

Keep in mind that just because something is in vogue doesn't mean that it will look good on you or appeal to men. Men don't necessarily care for the 'waif' look or like it when women wear long granny dresses and combat boots, however popular the look may be. They like women in feminine clothes. Wear a short skirt (but not too short), if you have the legs for it.

Also, don't feel that you have to wear designer clothes to attract men. Men don't care whose label you're wearing, just how your clothes look and fit on you. It's better to buy a no-name brand that looks stunning and hides your hips that a designer outfit that doesn't.

While you're shopping in a department store, stop by a cosmetics counter and treat yourself to a makeover. We can all look better than we do. Many of us don't realize our potential until we get a makeover, which, by the way, is often given for free with a minimal purchase. Pay attention to which colours are good for you and how the makeup artist applies them. Buy whatever he or she suggests that you can afford and go home and practise putting it on.

Don't leave the house without wearing makeup. Put lipstick on even when you go jogging!

Do everything you possibly can to put your best face forward. If you have a bad nose, get a nose job; colour grey hair; grow your hair long. Men prefer long hair, something to play with and caress. It doesn't matter what your hairdresser and friends think. You're certainly not trying to attract them! Let's face it, hairdressers are notorious for pushing exciting, short haircuts on their clients; trimming long hair is not fun for them. It doesn't matter that short hair is easier to wash and dry or that your hair is very thin. The point is, we're girls! We don't want to look like boys.

It will be easier to feel like a creature unlike any

other if you follow good grooming. Manicures, pedicures, periodic facials and massages should become part of your routine. And don't forget to spray on an intoxicating perfume when you go out – just don't overdo it.

Now that you look the part, you must act the part. Men like women. Don't act like a man, even if you are head of your own company. Let him open the door. Be feminine. Don't tell sarcastic jokes. Don't be a loud, knee-slapping, hysterically funny girl. This is okay when you're alone with your girlfriends. But when you're with a man you like, be quiet and mysterious, act ladylike, cross your legs and smile. Don't talk so much. Wear black sheer stockings and hike up your skirt to entice the opposite sex! You might feel offended by these suggestions and argue that this will suppress your intelligence or vivacious personality. You may feel that you won't be able to be yourself, but men will love it!

In addition, don't sound cynical or depressed and tell long-winded stories of all the people who have hurt you or let you down. Don't make your prospective husband a saviour or therapist. On the contrary, act as if you were born happy. Don't tell everything about yourself. Say thank you and please. Practise this ladylike behaviour with waiters, doormen and even cab drivers who take the long way to your destination. This will make it easier to be ladylike on dates.

If you never meet men accidentally, go to everything – dances, tennis parties (even if you don't play tennis), Club Med. Just go, go, go – show up! Put a personal ad in a magazine, answer ads, ask people to set you up. Don't shy away from singles events with the rationalization that 'The men who go there aren't my type.' Remember, you are not trying to find large groups of men who are your type, just one! Don't lose sight of this concept. It will keep you going on those bad days when you are convinced that true love is just never going to happen to you!

Last but not least, trust this process. You may not meet your husband immediately after you have got in shape, bought some terrific outfits and practised *The Rules* on three eligible men. It may not be your time. But it is our experience that if you continue to do *The Rules* at every opportunity and pray for patience, you will eventually meet and marry the man of your dreams.

5 | *The Rules*

Rule 1 _____

Be a 'Creature Unlike Any Other'

Being a creature unlike any other is a state of mind. You don't have to be rich, beautiful or exceptionally smart to feel this way about yourself. And you don't have to be born with this feeling either. It can be learned, practised and mastered, like all the other rules in this book.

Being a creature unlike any other is really an attitude, a sense of confidence and radiance that permeates your being from head to toe. It's the way you smile (you light up the room), pause in between sentences (you don't babble on and on out of nervousness), listen (attentively), look (demurely, never stare), breathe (slowly), stand (straight) and walk (briskly, with your shoulders back).

It doesn't matter if you're not a beauty queen, that

you never finished college or that you don't keep up with current events. You will think you're enough! You have more confidence than women with MBAs or money in the bank. You don't grovel. You're not desperate or anxious. You don't date men who don't want you. You trust in the abundance and goodness of the universe: if not him, someone better, you say. You don't settle. You don't chase anyone. You don't use sex to make men love you. You believe in love and marriage. You're not cynical. You don't go to pieces when a relationship doesn't work out. Instead, you get a manicure and go out on another date or to a singles dance. You're an optimist. You brush away a tear so that it doesn't smudge your makeup and you move on! Of course, that is not how you really *feel*. This is how you *pretend* you feel until it feels real. *You act as if*!

On a date, you never show that getting married is foremost on your mind. You're cool. He may think you've turned down several marriage proposals. You sip – never slurp – your drink and let him find out all about you, instead of the other way around. Your answers are short, light and flirtatious. Your gestures are soft and feminine. When your hair falls in front of your face, you tilt your head back and comb back your hair with your hand from the top of your head in a slow, sweeping motion.

All your movements – the way you excuse yourself to use the ladies room or look at your watch to end the date – are fluid and sexy, not jerky or self-conscious. You've been on many dates before; you're a pro. That's because you take care of yourself. You didn't lie in bed depressed, eating cakes before the date. You took a bubble bath, read this book and built up your soul with positive slogans like, 'I'm a beautiful woman. I am enough.' You told yourself that you don't have to do anything more on the date than show up. He'll either love you or not. It's not your fault if he doesn't call again. You're beautiful, inside and out. Someone else will love you if he doesn't. All that matters is that you end the date first (see *Rule 12*).

When you go to singles dances or parties, you pump yourself up. You pretend you're a movie star. You hold your head high and walk in as if you just flew in from New York on the Concorde. You're only in town for one night and if some lucky hunk doesn't swoop down and grab you it'll be his loss!

You get a drink, a Perrier perhaps, even if you're not thirsty. It keeps your hands busy so you don't bite your nails or twirl your hair out of nervousness. You don't show that you're nervous, even if you are. That's the secret: you act as if everything's great, even if you're on the verge of flunking college or getting fired. You walk briskly, as if you know where you're going, which is just around the room. You keep moving. You don't stand in a corner waiting for anyone. They have to catch you in motion.

If you think you aren't pretty, if you think other girls are better dressed or thinner or cooler, you keep it to yourself. You tell yourself, 'Any man would be lucky to have me', until it sinks in and you start to believe it. If a man approaches you, you smile and answer his questions very nicely without saying too much. You're demure, a bit mysterious. You leave him hungry for more, as opposed to bored. After a few minutes you say, 'I think I'll walk around now.'

Most women hang around men all night waiting to be asked to dance. But you do *The Rules*. If he wants to be with you or get your phone number, he'll search the crowded room until he finds you. You don't offer him *your* pen or business card. You don't make it easy for him. Don't even carry them with you or you may be tempted to 'help him out'. The reason is that *he* has to do all the work. As he scrambles around begging the coat-check girl for a pen, you stand by quietly. You think to yourself, '*The Rules* have begun!'

It's that simple. You do *The Rules* and trust that one day a prince will notice that you're different from all other women he's known, and ask for your hand!

Don't Talk to a Man First
(and Don't Ask Him to Dance)

Never? Not even 'Let's have coffee' or 'Do you come here often?' Right, not even these seemingly harmless openers. Otherwise, how will you know if he spotted you first, was smitten by you and had to have you, or is just being polite?

We know what you're thinking. We know how extreme such a rule must sound, not to mention snobbish, silly and painful; but taken in the context of *The Rules*, it makes perfect sense. After all, the premise of *The Rules* is that we never make anything happen, that we trust in the natural order of things – namely, that man pursues woman.

By talking to a man first, we interfere with whatever was supposed to happen or not happen, perhaps causing a conversation or a date to occur that was never meant to be and inevitably getting hurt in the process. Eventually, he'll talk to the girl he really wants and drop you.

Yet, we manage to rationalize this behaviour by telling ourselves, 'He's shy' or 'I'm just being friendly.' Are men really shy? We might as well tackle this question right now. Perhaps a therapist would say so, but we believe that most men are not shy, just not *really*, *really* interested if they don't approach you. It's hard to accept that, we know. It's also hard waiting for the right one – the one who talks to you first, calls and basically does most of the work in the beginning of the relationship because he must have you.

It's easy to rationalize women's aggressive behaviour in this day and age. Unlike years ago when women met men at dances and 'coming out' parties and simply waited for one to pick them out of the crowd and start a conversation, today many women are accountants, doctors, lawyers, dentists and in management positions. They work with men, for men, and men work for them. Men are their patients and their clients. How can a woman not talk to a man first?

The Rules answer is to treat men you are interested in like any other client or patient or co-worker, as hard as that might be. Let's face it, when a woman meets a man she really likes, a light bulb goes on in her head and she sometimes, without realizing it, relaxes, laughs and spends more time with him than is necessary. She may suggest lunch to discuss something that could be discussed over the phone because she is hoping to ignite some romance. This is a common ploy. Some of the smartest women try to make things happen under the guise of business. They think they are too educated or talented to be passive, play games or do *The Rules*. They feel their diplomas and salaries entitle them to do more in life than wait for the phone to ring. These women, we assure you, always end up heartbroken when their forwardness is rebuffed. But why shouldn't it be? Men know what they want. No one has to ask them to lunch.

So, the short of it is that if you meet men professionally, you still have to do *The Rules*. You must wait until he brings up lunch or anything else beyond business. As we explain in *Rule 22*, the man must take the lead. Even if you are making the same amount of money as a man you are interested in, he must bring up lunch. If you refuse to accept that men and women are different romantically, even though they may be equal professionally, you will behave like men – talk to them first, ask for their phone number, invite them to discuss the case over dinner at your place – and drive them away. Such forwardness is very risky; sometimes we have seen it work, most of the time it doesn't, and it *always* puts the woman through hell emotionally. By not accepting the concept that the man must pursue the woman, women put themselves in jeopardy of being rejected or ignored, if not at the moment, then at some point in the future. We hope you never have to endure the following torture:

Our dentist friend Pam initiated a friendship with Robert when they met in dental school several years ago by asking him out to lunch. *She spoke to him first.* Although they later became lovers and even lived together, he never seemed really 'in love' with her and her insecurity about the relationship never went away. Why would it? *She spoke to him first.* He recently broke up with her over something trivial. The truth is he never loved her. Had Pam followed *The Rules*, she would never have spoken to Robert or initiated anything in the first place. Had she followed *The Rules*, she might have met someone else who truly wanted her. She would not have wasted time. *Rules* girls don't waste time.

Here's another example of a smart woman who broke *The Rules*: Claudia, a confident Wall Street broker, spotted her future husband on the dance floor of a popular disco and planted herself next to him for a good five minutes. When he failed to make the first move, she told herself that he was probably shy or had two left feet and asked him to dance. The relationship has been filled with problems. She often complains that he's as 'shy' in the bedroom as he was that night on the dance floor.

A word about dances. It's become quite popular these days for women to ask men to dance. Lest there is any doubt in your mind, this behaviour is totally against *The Rules*. If a man doesn't bother to walk across the room to seek you out and ask you to dance, then he's obviously not interested and asking him to dance won't change his feelings or rather his lack of feelings for you. He'll probably be flattered that you asked and dance with you just to be polite and he might even want to have sex with you that night, but he won't be crazy about you. Either he didn't notice you or you made it too easy. He never got the chance to pursue you and this fact will always permeate the relationship even if he does ask you out.

We know what you're thinking: what am I supposed to do all night if no one asks me to dance? Unfortunately, the answer is to go to the bathroom five times if you have to, reapply your lipstick, powder your nose, order more water from the bar, think happy thoughts, walk around the room in circles until someone notices you, make phone calls from the lobby to your married friends for encouragement – in short, anything but ask a man to dance. Don't even stand next to someone you like, hoping he'll ask you, as many women do. You have to *wait* for someone to notice you. You might have to go home without having met anyone you liked or even danced one dance. But tell yourself that at least you got to practise *The Rules* and there's always another dance. You walk out with a sense of accomplishment that at least you didn't break *The Rules*!

If this sounds boring, remember the alternative is worse. Our good friend Sally got so resentful of having to dance with all the 'losers' at a particular party that she finally decided to defy *The Rules* she knew only too well and asked the best-looking man in the room to dance. Not only was he flattered, but they danced for hours and he asked her out for the next three nights. 'Maybe there are exceptions to *The Rules*,' she thought triumphantly. She found out otherwise, of course. It seems Mr Right was in town for just a few days on business and already had a girlfriend. No wonder he hadn't asked anyone to dance that night. He probably just went to the party to have fun, not to find his future wife. The moral of the story: don't figure out why someone hasn't asked you to dance – there's always a good reason.

Unfortunately, more women than men go to dances to meet 'The One'. Their eagerness and anxiety get the best of them and they end up talking to men first or asking them to dance. So you must condition yourself not to expect anything from a dance. View it simply as an excuse to put on high heels, apply a new shade of blush and be around a lot of people. Chances are someone of the opposite sex will start to talk to *you* at some point in the evening. If and when he does, and you're not having such a great time, don't show it. For example, don't be clever or cynical and say, 'I would have been better off staying home and watching *Friends*.' Men aren't interested in women who are witty in a negative way. If someone asks if you're having a good time, simply say yes and smile.

If you find all of this much too hard to do, then don't go to the dance. Stay home, do sit-ups, watch *Friends* and reread *The Rules*. It's better to stay home and read *The Rules* than go out and break them.

Don't Stare at Men or Talk Too Much

Looking at someone first is a dead give-away of interest. Let him look at *you*! If he doesn't notice you first, he's probably not interested. Keep walking, someone else will notice you.

Did you know that there are workshops designed to teach women how to make eye contact with men they find attractive? Save your money. It is never necessary to make eye contact. What about letting men know you're receptive? We suggest simply smiling at the room (or the universe, if you will) and looking relaxed and approachable. That's how to acknowledge a man's attention, not by staring at him. Don't look anxiously around for 'The One'. That is certain to make anyone look the other way. There is nothing attractive about anxiety.

On the first date, avoid staring romantically into his eyes. Otherwise, he will know that you're planning the honeymoon. Instead, look down at the table or your food, or simply survey the crowd at the restaurant. It's best to seem generally interested in life, in others, in your surroundings, in the paintings on the wall, as opposed to this live prey. He will feel crowded and self-conscious if you gaze at him too much. Restrain yourself. Let him spend the evening trying to get *your* attention.

One of the hardest aspects of dating is figuring out what to say. Do you talk about the weather or politics? Should you be intellectual or girlish? If you're smart, you'll stay cool and just listen to what he says. Follow his lead. If he wants to talk about dance clubs, tell him which one's you've been to and which ones you like. We're not suggesting that you be an airhead. On the contrary! It's just that you're easy to be with. When appropriate, show him that you keep up with current events and have interests.

Early dating is *not* the time to tell him about your job problems. In general, don't be too heavy. But don't be funny if he's serious. Just go with the flow.

Needless to say, there will be moments on a date when neither of you has anything to say. Don't feel the need to fill in these silences. You'll end up saying something stupid and forced. Sometimes men just want to drive in silence without saying a word. Let them. Maybe he's thinking about how he's going to propose to you one day. Don't ruin his concentration.

Don't feel you have to be entertaining or have interesting conversation all the time. He will think you are trying too hard. Just be there! Remember, men fall in love with your essence, not with anything in particular you say.

If anything, men should be the ones scrambling their brains to come up with clever lines, asking you a lot of questions, and wondering whether or not they're keeping you interested. Besides, most men find chatty women annoying. We know one man who stopped calling a woman he was physically attracted to because she simply didn't stop talking. Don't be like that. As a woman, you probably like to talk, *especially* about the relationship, but you must hold your tongue. Wait until the date is over and then you can call ten girlfriends and analyse the date for hours.

On the date itself, be quiet and reserved. He'll wonder what you're thinking, if you like him, and if he's making a good impression. He'll think you're interesting and mysterious, unlike many of the women he's dated. Don't you want him to think about you like that?

Don't Meet Him Halfway
or Go Dutch on a Date

Men love a challenge – that's why they play sports, fight wars and raid corporations. The worst thing you can do is make it easy for them. When a man is trying to set up a date to meet you, don't say, 'Actually, I'm going to be in your area anyway'; don't offer the names of restaurants between your place and his, unless he asks. Don't say much at all. Let him do all the thinking, the talking, let him flip through the Yellow Pages or magazine listings and call a couple of friends for suggestions to come up with a place convenient for you. Men really feel good when they work hard to see you. Don't take that away from them.

The Rule is that men are supposed to rearrange their schedules around you, pursue you, take cabs and trains to see you. For example, on their second date, Charles drove forty miles out of his way to see Michele because she was spending the weekend at her mother's. Most girls would have left their mums in the lurch so that their date wouldn't have to be inconvenienced. But Michele was schooled in *The Rules* and knew the right thing to do. The extra miles only made Charles more determined to see her.

Friends and colleagues meet halfway. Men (real men) pick up women at their homes or offices for dates. Always make the place convenient for you. We don't care where you live.

Invariably, we find that men who insist that their dates meet them halfway or (worse) on their own turf, turn out to be turds – inconsiderate, uncompromising and even miserly. Jane recalls that after cabbing across town to meet Steve (a blind date) at his favourite brunch place, he suggested they split the bill.

Jane, a truly nice person, agreed that it was only fair to pay her share. After all, she made a considerable amount of money as a lawyer and felt it would be 'unfair' for Steve to 'absorb' the entire cost of the date. Why should he have to pick up the whole tab? That was very nice of Jane, but we assure you that had she insisted that they meet at a place near her, perhaps just for a drink (especially if she didn't feel right spending his money), Steve would have treated her like a princess, not a co-worker. But since Jane made everything so easy for him, he didn't treat her well, lost interest, and eventually stopped calling.

It's not that women aren't capable of taking public transport and paying for themselves. It's just chivalrous, hence *The Rules*, for men to pick up their dates and pick up the bills. Equality and Dutch treat are fine in the workplace, but not in the romantic playing field. Love is *easy* when the man pursues the woman and pays for the woman most of the time. He feels that the money he spends on the food, the movie and the cabs is the

33

price of being with you and it's worth every penny. You should feel honoured, happy, not guilty.

But if part of you feels uncomfortable about him paying for everything, offer to leave a tip or, if the night is a long one – say dinner, a show and three cab rides or parking – pay for something small along the way. But don't pay for anything on the first three dates. Later on, you can reciprocate in your own way: cook him dinner at your place or buy him a baseball cap. If he's on a tight budget or is a student and you're worried about him spending tuition money, still don't split the bill. Instead, suggest inexpensive places to eat and have a hamburger. Don't order appetisers or more than one drink. There's always pizza or Chinese food. Suggest movies, museums and cheap outdoor concerts.

It's nice of you to care about his finances, but remember that he is deriving great pleasure from taking you out. Why deprive him of the joy of feeling chivalrous? Actually, the best way you can repay him is by being appreciative. Say thank you and please. Don't criticize the place or the food or the service, even if they are plain awful. Be positive. Look for the good in everything. We know one man who became even more enamoured of a girl on their second date because she didn't complain one word when he couldn't remember where he parked at a football game. For the whole hour during which they pounded the pavement looking for his car, he kept thinking, 'What a great girl!'

Many things can go wrong on a date, especially when a guy is so eager to impress you that he ends up making more mistakes – locking his keys in the car, forgetting the theatre tickets and so on. Never use these blunders to make him feel bad. Instead, see all the effort and expense he is putting into the date. Being a good sport could make the difference between being just another date and his future wife.

Don't Call Him and Rarely Return His Calls

If you are following *The Rules* religiously, there is no reason to call him. He should be calling you, and calling you again and again until he pins you down for a date.

To call men is to pursue them, which is totally against *The Rules*. They will immediately know that you like them and possibly lose interest! Another reason not to call men is so you don't catch them in the middle of something — watching a football game, paying bills, entertaining a friend or even sleeping — when they may not be in the mood to talk to you. Why take a chance?

Invariably, when *you* call him, he will get off the phone first or quickly and you might misinterpret his busyness as disinterest. *You* may even think that he's with another woman! Understandably, you feel empty and nervous for the rest of the day or evening or until you hear from him again. This nervousness might make you call him again to ask, 'Is everything okay?' or 'Do you still love me? Miss me?' And, you end up breaking more rules!

So, if you don't want a man to know how much you like him, or that you feel empty and insecure, don't call him. If he leaves a message on your machine to return his call, try not to. Only call him back right away if it's a scheduling change regarding an upcoming date or event, not just to chat.

Not calling will leave him desiring you more, make him want to see you again and call you again. It prevents him from getting to know all about you much too quickly and getting bored. Besides, when you call only once in a while, it becomes special.

Don't worry about seeming rude. When he loves you or wants to get in touch with you badly, he won't think you're rude, just busy or hard to get – and men always call again.

Have you ever noticed that the conversation is always better when men call you? That's because when they call you, they're doing the dialling, they want you, miss you at that moment and can't wait to hear your voice. When they call you, they're the aggressor, they've thought about what they're going to say and have made the time to say it. They're available!

The Rules work for you when they call you because you may not be home and they'll wonder where you are or have to call again. When they call you, you might be busy and have to nicely cut the conversation short. It will be easier to do *Rule 6: Always End Phone Calls First*, when you let them call you.

But none of us are saints, and the reality is that we sometimes have to call men back. Not call them, mind you, just call them back. If, for whatever reason, you have to return a man's calls, try to wait. Don't call right back. When you do, keep the conversation short and sweet. Don't tell his machine what time and what nights you can be reached or volunteer any additional information about how he can reach you. That would be making it too easy for him and you will appear too eager. Let him figure it out! Remember, you're a *Rules* girl and you're very busy! A *Rules* girl typically comes home to many messages on her answering machine from men trying to fill up her weekends.

Now what if he leaves a message on your machine on Tuesday night and you're dying to get a Saturday night date out of him? Do you call back Tuesday night? *The Rules* answer is no because it will seem obvious that you are probably calling to get a Saturday night date. Better that *he* call *you* again by Wednesday night (the absolute cut-off) for a Saturday night date. Better not to have a date on Saturday night than to get in the habit of calling him. *The Rules* are not about getting a date, but a husband. Don't win the battle and lose the war.

Remember, *The Rules* are also about not getting hurt or dumped. We never want you to go through unnecessary pain. Life has enough pain without our adding man pain to it. We can't control cancer or drunk drivers, but we can restrain ourselves from dialling his number. If you call him and he doesn't return your call or doesn't ask you out, you'll be crushed. If you call him, he'll think you're not so elusive and he won't have to work so hard. If you call him, he won't get trained to ask you out at the end of each date. He has to learn that if he doesn't ask you out when he sees you, he might not reach you on the phone so soon and not see you for a week or two. It's not that you're *impossible* to get, you're just *hard* to get. Remember, you're very busy with activities and other dates and you make plans ahead of time. But don't reprimand him for not calling sooner by saying, 'If you had called earlier…' Just say, 'Really, I'd love to, but I can't'. (He'll figure out he has to call sooner).

If he's in love with you, he'll start calling Monday or Tuesday for Saturday night. If he doesn't love you, then he won't call you again and again until he pins you down.

However, don't be surprised if a man takes a week or two after the first date to call. He may have a lot of things going on or he may be dating other women. He may be trying to fit you into his schedule but just isn't sure how to do it. Remember, he had a life before he met you! Don't flip out! Just get busy (so you don't think about him twenty-four hours a day). Give him space, wait for *him* to call.

Here's a good example of how to handle such a situation: Our friend Laura waited two and a half weeks after her first date with David to hear from him. David was newly divorced and needed time to think before jumping into another relationship. A *Rules* girl, Laura gave him time and space. Unlike most women, she didn't call to 'see how he was doing' or with some other excuse like, 'Didn't you say you needed the name of my financial planner?' Sure, Laura was hurt, but she made plans with friends and went on blind dates. She had a pragmatic attitude. She knew that if he liked her, he'd eventually call; if he didn't, it was his loss! *Next!* When David finally called, she was nice and friendly. She didn't demand to know why he didn't call sooner and want to *talk* about it. They dated for ten months and are married now.

One last thought about the phone: sometimes we want to call a man we are dating not to speak to him, but just to hear his voice. We feel that we are simply going to die if we don't hear his sexy voice this minute! That's understandable. We suggest you call his home answering machine when he's at work. Hang up before the beep. It really works!

Always End Phone Calls First

Don't call men (see *Rule 5*), except occasionally to return their calls. When a man calls you, don't stay on the phone for more than ten minutes. Buy a timer if you have to. When the bell rings, you have to go! That way you seem busy and you won't give away too much about yourself or your plans (even if you don't have any plans). By ending the conversation first, you leave them wanting more. Good conversation enders are: 'I have a million things to do,' 'Well, it's been really nice talking to you,' 'Actually, I'm kind of busy right now,' and 'My beeper's beeping, got to run!' Remember to say these things in a very nice way.

Women love to talk. And one of their biggest faults is talking to men as if they were their girlfriends, therapists or next-door neighbours. Remember, early on in a relationship, the man is the adversary (if he's someone you really like). He has the power to hurt you by never calling again, by treating you badly or by being around but indifferent. While it's also true that you can reject him, the fact is that it's the man who notices you, asks you out and ultimately proposes marriage. He runs the show. The best way to protect yourself from pain is to not get emotionally involved too quickly.

So don't stay on the phone for an hour or two recounting your feelings or every incident of the day. You'll become transparent very quickly and run the risk of making him tired or bored. He does not want to date his crazy younger sister, his chatterbox mother or his gossipy next-door neighbour. He wants to talk to a girl who's friendly, light and breezy. By getting off the phone first, you don't have to wonder if you've kept him on too long, bored him or revealed too much about yourself. Because it can be very difficult to monitor the amount of time you spend on the phone when you are 'in like' or in love, we again suggest using a timer or stopwatch. When the bell rings, you sweetly say, 'I really have to go now.' A timer is objective; you are not.

It doesn't matter if you're having a great conversation and you want to tell him all about what happened to you between the ages of five and six that shaped your life. When the bell rings, the conversation is over. Remember, you always want to be mysterious. Having to get off the phone first creates a certain amount of mystery in his mind. He'll wonder why you have to go so soon, what you're doing, and if you're dating someone else. It's good for him to wonder about you. *The Rules* (and a timer) will make him wonder about you a lot.

You may think that men will find your abruptly ending a phone call rude and won't call again. On the contrary, just the opposite often happens simply because men are irrational when it comes to love. For example, our friend Janet set her timer to four minutes one evening. 'Got to go,' she said at the sound of the bell. Five minutes later he called back to insist that they start seeing each other twice a week instead of once a week. The four-minute call worked like a charm, bringing him closer to her, not (as you would expect) farther away.

If you're a genuinely nice person, you will probably feel cruel when you do *The Rules*. You may think you are making men suffer, but in reality you are actually doing them a favour. By doing *The Rules*, you make men want to spend more time with you on the phone and in person. They get to experience longing! Tell yourself you are doing them a favour when you feel heartless about doing *The Rules*!

Another tip for driving a man to madness is to turn off your answering machine on a Sunday afternoon and see if he doesn't go crazy trying to pin you down. When Cindy tried this tactic, her boyfriend ended up calling so many times that day that he activated her answering machine. (Some machines will automatically turn on after fourteen rings. Can you imagine him letting it ring fourteen times?!) When he finally got her on the phone that night, he possessively asked, 'Where have you been? I wanted to take you for a drive in the country.' It's good when men get upset; it means they care about you. If they're not angry, they're indifferent, and if they're indifferent, they've got one foot out the door. Getting off the phone after a few minutes is not easy, but it works.

Our friend Kate felt that she was 'losing' Jeff, her boyfriend of three months, when after a Saturday night date he said good-bye very casually and told her, 'I'll call you. I'll let you know what's a good night for *me* next week'. Kate felt the tables turning and took an extreme but necessary *Rules* action. She didn't answer her phone the night he usually called. She just listened to it ring and ring. When he finally reached her the next day at work, he was a little less cocky and somewhat nervous. He asked her what night would be good for *her!* The phone strategy worked – he never pulled another stunt like that again.

Here's another phone tip: if you're home on a Friday night because you're tired or don't have a date, leave the answering machine on or have your mum or room-mate say you're not home. That way, if by some chance he calls you on a Friday night because he's not doing anything either, he'll think you're not home. The worst thing you can do is give him the impression that you aren't busy and sought after by other men. Don't let him think that you're a couch potato, even if you are. Don't think playing games is bad. Sometimes game playing is good. Men like to think that they are getting a catch. Show him that you have a full life, that you are independent.

On any other night when he calls and you pick up the phone, don't feel you have to tell him exactly what you are doing. After a few minutes, just say you're busy (nicely) and can't talk anymore. You won't be lying because sometimes you are busy – doing the laundry; just don't tell him you're doing the laundry. Never let him think, even if it's true, that you are home thinking about him and making the wedding guest list. Men love the seemingly unattainable girl!

Lest you think this advice is old-fashioned, remind yourself that you are a very fulfilled person – stable, functional and happy – with a career, friends and hobbies, and that you are perfectly capable of living with or without him. You are not an empty vessel waiting for him to fill you up, support you or give you a life. You are alive and enthusiastic, engaged in work and in living fully on your own. Men like women who are their own person, not needy leeches waiting to be rescued. *The Rules* are not about being rescued!

In fact, the biggest mistake a woman can make when she meets a man she wants to marry is to make him the centre of her life. She may jeopardize her job by daydreaming at her desk about Prince Charming, rather than rolling up her sleeves and working. All she thinks about and talks about is him. She bores her girl-friends to death with details about every date. She is constantly looking for ties to buy him or clipping newspaper articles that he would find interesting. Not only is such behaviour unhealthy, but also it's the surest way to lose him.

First of all, he may be overwhelmed by all the attention. Second, he may never propose. And third, he may never rescue you emotionally and financially in the way you think. Even if he marries you, he may always have that night out with the boys, his hobbies or that Sunday morning basketball game. And he may want a working wife. So better get used to the idea now that you must have a life of your own – a job, interests, hobbies, friends that you can fill up on in between dates and even when you are married. The worst thing you can do when dating is to expect him to be your entertainment director. Don't call him just because you're bored or want attention. Be happy and busy. He should always be catching you coming or going.

We hear again and again about women whose worlds shrink when they meet Mr Right. When you meet Mr Right is precisely the time to take up tennis, get an MBA or go on that camping trip with your friends.

If He Doesn't Call, He's Not That Interested. Period!

We know this is hard to accept. We've heard it all – every rationalization imaginable used to avoid having to confront this unpleasant truth: he said he was going to call at the end of the last date, but didn't. Now you're sure it's because you didn't smile or talk enough, or you talked too much. You didn't thank him for dinner. You ordered the most expensive dish and now he thinks you're after his money.

Or he hasn't called because he's busy, or he's going through something with his father or ex-wife. Business is rough and that's why he hasn't called.

He thought you didn't have a good time on the last date, so he didn't call.

He hasn't called because he lost your number.

We can come up with 100 reasons why a man didn't call. But the bottom line is, if he hasn't called, he's not that interested.

We're not saying he doesn't like you or that you didn't have a great date or that you're not on his mind sometimes, but if he hasn't actually dialled your number, how interested can he be?

If you have to call him to remind him you exist,

something is wrong. Then, if you pursue him and he ever marries you, you'll have to remind him it's your birthday or your wedding anniversary or call him at work to get his attention. You might have to initiate sex and holidays. You'll always have to be the one to call the travel agent because he may think about holidays, but he never gets around to calling. Things are the way they are! This is not the kind of relationship a *Rules* girl wants to get involved in.

So don't waste time analysing what you may have done to discourage him from calling. Let it go. No matter what the reason, if he doesn't call, it's *next*!

Don't Accept a Saturday Night
Date After Wednesday

It's quite common these days for men to ask women out
for the same night or the very next day. And it's equally
common for women to accept such casual, last-minute
invitations out of fear that it will be the best offer they
get that week. But this is not a *Rules* date. The man who
eventually wants to marry you will not wait until the
last minute to ask you out. On the contrary, he is kind,
considerate, thoughtful and also afraid that if he doesn't
pin you down five days in advance, he may not see you
for another week. And when he is in love with you, a
week will feel like eternity!

Needless to say, men don't always know they
shouldn't be calling you on Thursday or Friday night
for a Saturday night date. Other women have spoiled
them by accepting last-minute offers. As we've stated,
ideally he should ask you out at the end of your last date
or call you as early as Monday or Tuesday for the next
Saturday night. The *Rules* will make you foremost on
his mind, the first thing he thinks about in the morning.
And if you are always on his mind, he won't want to
wait until Thursday to call you.

It may be a telltale sign of how a man feels about you

if he doesn't call you early in the week. The best way to encourage him to phone sooner is to turn him down when he calls on Thursday for Saturday night. Hopefully, he will get the hint. This is not a game. It is essential that men ask you out early in the week because, as a *Rules* woman, you simply can't put your life on hold until Thursday or Friday! You have friends and lots of things to do. You need to know ahead of time if you're going to have a date Saturday night or go to the movies with the girls. When men are calling you as late as Thursday, you become a nervous wreck. You're frenetically checking your answering machine, or if you live at home, you're constantly asking your mother if he called. Basically, you're living on the edge. *Rules* girls don't live on the edge. They have plans.

If he hasn't called by Wednesday night, make other plans for the weekend. Then you must politely decline if he calls Thursday and nonchalantly asks, 'Hey, pet, what are you doing Saturday night?'

Practise the following answer in the nicest voice possible: 'Oh, I'm so sorry, but I've already made plans.' Don't break down and go out with him even though you'd much rather do that than hang out with the girls or go out with another man you don't like as much. And don't counteroffer by saying, 'But I'm free Monday.' Men have to ask you out without your help. *But don't reprimand him for calling so late in the week.* Be very nice, but very firm when you say no. Also, don't say what your plans are because it doesn't matter. What matters is the message you're sending, which is: If you want to get a Saturday night date with me, you must call on Monday, Tuesday or Wednesday.

Now you may be saying to yourself, 'This is all so rigid, lots of men make plans when the mood strikes them, what's wrong with spontaneity?' These arguments sound convincing, but the reality is not so pleasant. When Ted first called our friend Beth on a Thursday night for a Saturday night date, she said yes right away. That set a bad precedent for him calling her at the last minute for future dates. Although they went out for a few months, he never thought that much about her during the week and she felt confused by the relationship because she was never sure if she was going to see him Saturday night.

Remember, *The Rules* are about the long haul. The way a man behaves – rather, the way you *allow* him to behave toward you – during your courtship is usually the way he will behave during your marriage. For example, if he's last minute about dating you, he'll be last minute and inattentive about you in other ways. That's why last-minute dates are just unacceptable. Men who call ten minutes before they're going to be in your area to see you may be terrific dates, but how busy and hard to get are you if they can see you in ten minutes? If you give in, these men will end up treating you like someone they *can get* in ten minutes.

But remember to be very nice when you say no. Don't think negatively, 'This man doesn't think much of me to call right before he wants to see me.' Or scream, 'No, I'm busy,' and slam down the phone. He isn't thinking that at all. He isn't thinking that he's not treating you like a creature unlike any other. Give him a break. *Rules* girls are an unusual breed. As we've suggested, nicely say, 'No, wow, I wish I wasn't busy!' Then sigh and get off the phone. He will soon realize that you simply want to be asked in advance for a date. Again, men are not trying to hurt you when they call at the last minute. Don't be offended, just train them to call earlier without actually *demanding* it of them.

Spontaneity is not 'Hi. Want to see a movie this afternoon?' That call might have come out of boredom or the fact that the woman he really wants to be with is busy. He didn't call you in advance, dream about you for a week, and get all excited about putting his arm around your shoulders during the movie. He didn't think of your date together as something precious that must be scheduled in advance like a reservation at a very exclusive restaurant. Spontaneity is fine, but it should happen *during* the date, such as an unexpected drive to the beach after dinner.

We often hear about 'spontaneous' women who go out with men on twenty-four hours' notice. We wish them luck. When a man knows he can have you five minutes after his last girlfriend gave him the boot, he'll call you because he's lonely or bored, not because he's crazy about you. In such cases, buyer beware: it won't last. Free spirits might object to what we are saying, but for long-lasting results we believe in treating dating like a job, with rules and regulations. Just like you have to work from nine to five, no matter how you *feel*, we believe you have to silently train men to make plans with you (elusive, busy, happy you!) ahead of time. When you do *The Rules*, what you're really doing is giving men the secret, silent code that they understand very well. If you make it too easy for men, they're certain to take advantage and then you can forget about getting a *Rules* marriage.

We realize that the days in between dates with the man you are crazy about can be long and excruciating; but, remember, it's worse to say yes indiscriminately whenever he wants to see you and risk him getting bored. If you play your cards right, he will reach the conclusion that the only way to see you whenever he wants, at the last minute, is to marry you!

_____

Fill Up Your Time Before the Date

Most women go on dates with a lot of expectations. They want the man to find them beautiful, to ask them out again and to father their children. Needless to say, these women are usually disappointed. That's why we have found it very helpful – in fact, essential – to be booked up as much as possible before the date. It's best to be busy right up until the doorbell rings so that you're slightly breathless and brimming with energy when you finally see him.

Here are some suggestions for what to do on the day of the date:

1. To relieve anxiety, go to the gym, get a manicure or take a long hot bubble bath.
2. Buy a new shirt or a bottle of perfume. Get a makeover. Treat yourself.
3. Take a nap. If you're the type who gets drowsy at 10 p.m., a good nap will keep you going.
4. Go to the movies (see a comedy, not a romance, so love isn't too much on your mind), read the newspaper or a book to fill your head with something other than how your first name sounds with his last

name. If you're busy all day, you won't be so needy and empty when he picks you up.

Here's what *not* to do:

1. Don't talk to your girlfriends all day long about the date, about how his astrological sign and yours go together, about how you know he's 'The One', or about relationships in general. You really shouldn't be thinking about the date at all.

2. Don't see your mother, grandmother, or anyone who absolutely can't wait for you to get married and have children. Being around them might make you reek of desperation on the date. You might inadvertently mention the *M* word (marriage) and scare him away.

3. Don't write your name and his in all different combinations, such as:

Susan Johnson
Susan Dobbs Johnson
Susan D. Johnson

Don't you have better things to do?

How to Act on Dates 1, 2 and 3

If you are anything like us, you've thought a lot about how much the two of you have in common before he even arrives to pick you up. And you've named the children before he says hello. This type of seemingly innocuous daydreaming before the date is dangerous, possibly the worst thing you can do short of professing love to him during dessert. This kind of fantasising leads to unfulfilled longing and to unrealistic expectations of romance and passion that makes you prone to say foolish things like, 'I have two tickets to a concert,' after the first date. (Yes, you can reciprocate but much later – see *Rule 4*).

If at all possible, don't think of him before he arrives – it isn't necessary for the first three dates. Be busy right up until the minute he buzzes you from downstairs. Don't have him come up to your flat on the first date. Preferably, meet him downstairs or at a restaurant. (*Rules* girl play it safe.) On these three dates, don't tell him all about your day as if you've known each other for years, thinking that it will bring you closer. Don't be too serious, controlling or wifey. Don't mention the *M* word, not even to mention that your brother recently got married.

Remember that you are a creature unlike any other, a beautiful woman, inside and out. So don't feel that you have to fit in a love seminar or last-minute therapy session to be in good form. You should feel no pressure whatsoever.

In fact, all you really have to do on the first three dates is show up, relax, pretend you're an actress making a cameo appearance in a movie. Reread *Rule 1: Be a 'Creature Unlike Any Other'*. Be sweet and light. Laugh at his jokes, but don't try too hard. Smile a lot, and don't feel obligated to fill up the lulls in the conversation. In general, let him do all the work – pick you up, pick the restaurant, open the door, and pull out the chair. Act nonchalantly at all times, as if you're always on dates and it's nothing out of the ordinary (even if you haven't had a date in years). If you have to think about something, think about your date with another man that week. You should always try to date other people so that you never get hung up on one man at any time.

End the date first (see *Rule 12*), especially if you like him. Glance at your watch after two hours (for a drink date) or three or four hours (for a dinner date), simply sigh, and say, 'Well, this was really great, but I've got a really big day tomorrow.' Don't say what it is you're doing tomorrow. At the end of the first date, you can accept a light peck on the cheek or lips even though you're dying to do more.

Don't invite him up to your place at the end of the first date. After all, he's still a stranger at this point. He should only see the outside of your house. This is both for safety and *The Rules*. By not letting him into your flat or agreeing to go to his, you drastically reduce your chances of any sort of problem occurring. If you meet someone at a bar or party, the same rule applies. Don't get into his car for any reason (or you might end up in his boot!). Don't invite him to go to your flat or go to his that night. It's a crazy world out there. Play it safe!

On the second date, use your judgement. If you feel comfortable with this man, he can pick you up at your flat and you can invite him up for a drink at the end of the night. But when in doubt, meet him downstairs in the hall and say goodnight there as well. *Rules* girls don't take chances!

We know we're asking you to go against your feelings here, but you want to get married, don't you? Anyone can get a one-night stand. In summary, the first three dates should be like 'being and nothingness'. Dress nice, be nice, good-bye and go home. Not too much feeling, investment or heart. You're probably wondering how long you can keep up this act, right? Don't worry, it gets easier!

How to Act on Dates 4 Through Commitment Time

On the first three dates, you showed up and acted sweet. On the fourth date, you can show more of yourself. You can talk about your feelings, as long as you don't get too heavy, or play therapist or mother. Exhibit warmth, charm and heart. If his dog died or his football team lost, express sympathy. Look into his eyes, be attentive and a good listener so that he knows you are a caring human being – a person who would make a supportive wife. Still, don't mention words like *marriage, wedding, kids*, or *the future*. Those are subjects for him to bring up. He must take the lead. Talk about something outside your relationship, like your favourite sport, TV show, a great movie, the novel you just finished, an interesting article from the *Spectator* or a good museum exhibition you just saw. You get the idea!

Don't tell him what your astrologist, nutritionist, personal trainer, shrink or yoga instructor think about your relationship with him.

Don't tell him what a mess you were before you met him.

Don't tell him he's the first man to treat you with respect. He'll think you're a loser or a tramp.

Don't give him the third degree about his past relationships. It's none of your business.

Don't say, 'We've got to talk' in a serious tone, or he'll bolt from the bar stool.

Don't overwhelm him with your career triumphs. Try to let *him* shine.

Don't plague him with your neuroses!!

Remember, you won't have to keep such things to yourself forever. Just for the first few months ... until he says he's in love with you. Eventually you will become more of yourself. It's the first impression from the first few months of dating that men remember forever.

If you find it hard to keep up this act, then end the date early or see less of him. Letting it all hang out too soon is counterproductive to your goals. Many women are conditioned to open up very soon. This is fine for therapy or with a girlfriend, but don't do this on a date. *The Rules* are about opening up slowly so that men aren't overwhelmed by us. It's rather selfish and inconsiderate to burden people with our whole lives on a three-hour date, don't you think? Remember, *The Rules* are innately unselfish.

But not so unselfish that you feel you have to answer any question you regard as too personal or none of his business just yet. Don't tell him anything that you will regret. Some men like to pry secrets out of women. Women sometimes reveal more than they really care to, hoping that their revelations will draw a man closer to them – but afterwards they feel naked, as well as tricked and cheated. Better to smile when asked a question that is too personal and say, 'Oh, I'd rather not talk about that right now.'

Of course, personal matters may come up. Be careful how you answer his questions. If he asks you how long you are planning to live in your flat say you're renewing your lease. Don't say, for example, that you've been hoping to meet a man soon so that you can get a bigger flat with him when your lease is up. Even if that is in fact your true hope and desire, don't say so or your date will run to the nearest exit.

Act independent so that he doesn't feel that you're expecting him to take care of you. That's as true on the first date as the fiftieth. Jill remembers that when she went bed shopping for herself with Bruce, her boyfriend of six months, she deliberately bought a single bed rather than a queen-size bed. It killed her to have to do this as she was hoping he was 'The One' and knew if they were to get engaged and married she would have no use for the bed. But the foldout couch she'd been sleeping on was broken. Rather than consulting Bruce on the bed purchase – asking him what kind of bed he liked and what size he liked, as if to suggest that this might be the bed they would be sharing one day – she bought the single bed as if she had no intention of getting married soon.

It was important not to let Bruce know that she was buying a bed with him in mind, when they weren't married and might never be. Of course, the single bed hasn't gone to waste: Jill's in-laws (Bruce's parents) now keep it as a spare in their guest room.

Always End the Date First

If you have not been living by *The Rules*, then you probably didn't know that the first date or two should last no more than five hours. A good way to end the date is to nonchalantly glance at your watch and say something like, 'Gosh, I really must be going now. I have such a busy day tomorrow.' (As we said before, don't say what you're doing. It doesn't matter and it's none of his business.)

Ending the date first is not so easy when you really like him and want to marry him, and you're both having a great time. But it must be done because you must leave him wanting more of you, not less. If he wants to know more about you as the date is ending, he can always call you the next day or ask you out again when he drops you off. It is our experience that men will want to see you a lot, sometimes every day in the beginning, and then grow very bored very quickly. So abide by *The Rules* and he'll stay smitten.

Not ending the date first is bad enough. What's worse, however, is prolonging the date once it should have been over. Emily felt that she was 'losing' Bob at the end of their second date (dinner and movie), so she suggested that they go dancing. Bob didn't want to hurt her feelings so he said okay, then he never called again. Of course, Emily should have ended the date right after the movie, but she thought she could excite Bob with her great disco dancing.

Other women try to prolong a first or second date, for example, by inviting the man up to her flat for a drink or coffee so that he'll fall in love with her decorating, or her home-brewed decaf. No! First of all, it should be *the man* trying to prolong the date, not you. He should be suggesting dancing, drinks or a cafe where the two of you can get dessert and cappuccino. If he didn't suggest it, then it's not supposed to happen. Instead of worrying about making the date interesting or longer, just make sure you end it first.

Show Up Even If You Don't
Feel Like It

Some women are lucky. They marry their school or college sweetheart at twenty-two and never have to deal with dating again. But what if that's not your story and the only man in your life is your dry cleaner? You had some relationships in the past but they didn't work out because you didn't know about *The Rules*.

There are many women in your situation. They simply never meet men. Years go by without a Saturday night date. They spend New Year's Eve with girl-friends, Chinese takeout or a rented video.

Obviously you can't do *The Rules* if there are no men in your life. Don't despair – instead, focus on doing some-thing – anything – to increase your chances of meeting men so you can practise *The Rules* and get married.

A good rule to start is to carry out one social action per week, *no matter what!* Here are some suggestions:

Plan to go to a singles party this weekend, get involved in a church/synagogue social event, do charity work or work on a political campaign where you might meet men, book a trip to Club Med, place a personal ad, join a dating service, take a share in a ski house or summer beach house, play tennis, jog around the park in your neighbourhood, anything! You don't have to dance well, campaign well, ski well, play tennis well or jog very far. You just have to plan these activities, show up, do your best and smile.

Perhaps you are thinking, 'But I don't have anyone to go with.' Then you *must* go alone! Of course, it would be great to have a friend (with similar interests) to go with, but if you don't have one, that's no excuse to sit at home. Many women we know actually pushed themselves to go alone to a party or social affair when they absolutely didn't want to go, and those were the very nights they met their husbands.

If you keep waiting for someone to go with, a convenient ride to the event or the perfect weather, you might never go. How serious are you about meeting someone if you won't go by yourself? Sometimes it's actually *better* to go alone because you're on your own time schedule and some men find you easier to approach.

Besides, you must learn to accept that, as an adult, you can't always rely on a friend to do things with. There are many tasks in life that have to be done alone, such as going on job interviews or going to the dentist. Sometimes you have to think about social activities at work — you have to do them regardless of how you feel.

Motivating yourself to get off the couch, dress, put on makeup and show up won't be easy, but it must be done. You may or may not have fun at the party, but at the very least, you'll practise *The Rules* for an hour or two and go home.

Don't think, 'But I'm not comfortable' at this or that. Go anyway!

We know it's not comfortable to be single in social gatherings, but then again, many things we tell you to do in *The Rules* are not always comfortable. You're also probably worrying that the kind of men you're attracted to won't come up to you, or that you'll be frustrated because you can't approach them since you're doing *The Rules*. You may not feel that you will have a good time and that you might have had more fun reading a good book in bed, but you'll never meet anyone that way, so you have to go!

Even if you don't meet Mr Right, going out — whether it be to an 'in' restaurant, museum, lecture or party — is good for you. It's a chance to meet new people, broaden your horizons, learn to be at ease in crowds, and best of all, to practise *The Rules*.

Tell a friend that you're going to take one social action this week and make sure you stick to it!

Long-Distance Relationships.
Part I: How They Should Start

Many questions arise in long-distance relationships that don't come up when dating a man closer to home. But before going into the specific rules for these relationships, it's important to talk about the mistakes women make when they first meet a man from out-of-town — mistakes that can easily prevent a long-distance *Rules* relationship from ever developing. As we have said before, it's the first encounter — who spoke to whom first, how long the conversation lasted, and who ended it first — that often determines whether it's a *Rules* relationship or not.

Let's look at some typical scenarios:

You meet a man at a mutual friend's wedding in Manchester. You're from London and he's from Edinburgh. He comes up to you and asks you to dance. It's *The Rules*! You like him a lot. You dance one dance and then another and then another. You feel glued to his side.

You know you should really walk away, say hello to some college friends you haven't talked to in years, but you don't. You figure the two of you live miles apart, who knows if you'll ever see him again, so what's the harm with spending five hours with him?

He asks you to join him for dessert. You say yes. Then he invites you to take a walk with him around the grounds. You agree. He takes your phone number at the end of the evening, kisses you good-bye and says something about calling you in a few days, maybe visiting London.

You're in love. You go back home and tell your friends and your mother, and start thinking about your own wedding.

But because you broke *The Rules* by spending so much time with him, he either never calls, or calls after a week or two just to say hello but doesn't make plans to see you. Or he calls and invites you to visit him in Edinburgh, or makes plans to see you in London but only because he's going to be there on business anyway. Naturally, you feel hurt and disappointed. Why doesn't he sound crazy about you? Why doesn't he want to jump on a train and see you right away?

Looking back on the evening – and after reading *The Rules* – you realize that you didn't play hard to get. You spent five straight hours with him. He knew you liked him and the challenge was gone.

We're not saying that had you walked away or turned him down a couple of times for dances that he would definitely call and pursue a long-distance relationship. Maybe he has a girlfriend in Edinburgh, maybe he just wanted to have fun at the wedding – nothing more, nothing less.

But by *not* doing *The Rules*, you lessened your chances, you got your hopes up, and you got emotionally involved and hurt. If he was interested and you were more elusive, chances are he would have thought about you on the train journey home, missed you in Edinburgh, called sooner, and made plans to see you in London, even if he didn't have a business trip there.

In the future, when you meet someone at a wedding or party whom you may never see again, don't spend the entire evening with him. Talk to him for fifteen to twenty minutes, dance with him a couple of times, and then excuse yourself to use the ladies' room or say hello to a friend or just walk around for a while. He should be looking for you during the evening and trying to pin you down for another dance.

When you spend four or five hours with a man you just met, he no longer finds you as mysterious or interesting, even if he made the first move. When he goes back home, he may not think you're that special or dream about seeing you again because you were too available.

The same goes for meeting a man on a business trip. Let's say you meet a man at a conference. He notices you, strikes up a conversation and asks you to have dinner with him that evening since he's leaving town the next morning. You say yes because he's cute and maybe something will start. You tell yourself you may never cross paths again – you live hundreds of miles apart – and you weren't going to do anything special for dinner anyway but order room service and watch TV. *The Rules* answer is to say, 'Thank you, but I already have plans.' Why? Because if you see him at the last minute, even if it's convenient for both of you, some of the challenge evaporates. If he's interested in you, let him call you and make special plans to visit you. If he can see you at a moment's notice, he won't have to long for you and pursue you and whatever interest he had in you may fizzle.

Don't think we're being overly strict about this. We see it happen time and time again. A woman meets a man at a business function or a party who says he's in town for just a few days and wants to take her to dinner that very night. He's totally charming and makes her feel special. She tells herself that she would really be missing something if she turned him down. He won't be in town again for another month.

She says yes – maybe it's just dinner, maybe she sleeps with him – and she thinks this is the beginning of a whirlwind courtship.

The reality is, it may not be. He may be lying. He may be in town for another week, but figures this way he'll get what he wants right away. Or he may be married and this is his standard pick-up line when he's out of town. There are men who have a girl in every port. You don't want to be one of them. But even if he's sincere, single and really likes you, the answer is still no to a last-minute date. You think if you say no, he'll forget you. But *Rules* girls know that he'll remember you that much more if you turn him down.

So the next time you meet a man who asks you to dinner the same night because he's in town just a few days, say, 'I'd love to, but I have other plans.' Let him call you in advance the next time he plans to be in town or make a special trip to see you.

The only way to know if a man is really interested in you – instead of just filling up a few hours – is to not accept a last-minute date. When you make him wait several days to see you or you make him wait until he's in town again a month later, he gets to experience longing. If his feelings about you are just lukewarm, he won't bother to make a date beforehand – by following *The Rules*, you'll avoid wasting your time and having your hopes dashed later on.

Here's another common long-distance scenario. You meet Mr Right on the first day of a seven-day holiday. Perhaps you're from different cities and you meet on a Club Med trip. He speaks to you first, asks you out for that night, and wants to be with you for all seven days and nights. You think, why not? He's cute. This is the whirlwind romance you always read about and dreamed about.

In this situation, you *must* force yourself not to see this man for the whole trip. See him once or twice for dinner and dancing over the seven-day period, but turn him down to be with other people so that he finds you mysterious and elusive and is forced to pursue you when he returns home. If he doesn't call you after the trip, at least you didn't waste seven days and nights on a man who's not that interested.

We know men who go on such trips, pursue one woman the whole time, sleep with her and then never think about her (much less call her) again when they return home. Here, you're thinking this is true love, and he's thinking sex, sand and fun for a week. If you don't want to be nothing more than the girl he slept with in Club Med, don't see him more than once or twice that week and don't sleep with him, otherwise you'll be crushed if you never hear from him again. It'll be a classic case of 'I love you, honey, but the holiday's over.'

So, by doing *The Rules*, you won't throw away a whole week on someone who may not have serious intentions and you will be open to meeting other men. If he really likes you, he'll call you and visit you afterward.

Long Distance Relationships.
Part II: Making it Work

Assuming you're beginning or already in a long-distance relationship, what are *The Rules*?

You don't call him. He calls you. He can call you often, but make sure you don't spend endless hours on the phone. Leave something to talk about when he visits you! Get off the phone in fifteen or twenty minutes – you can talk longer than the standard ten minutes since it is long-distance – whether or not he talks about making plans to see you. If he wants to visit you on the weekend, he must ask you by Wednesday.

Chances are if he approached you, he'll suggest coming to visit you first, which is *The Rules*. But if he suggests that you meet him in his city, or in some place halfway, simply say, 'That sounds nice, but things are really hectic right now, I just couldn't get away.' Don't spell out what's hectic or exactly why you can't get away. Just say no nicely and he'll realize that he has to visit you.

If he decides not to make the trip, he didn't like you that much. Remember that men drive for hours to go to football games and gambling casinos or to their college roommate's bachelor party, so it's not a big deal if they have to drive for hours to visit you.

Better that you never see him again than you visit him first or even meet him halfway. Meeting him halfway is the same as visiting him – it's not *The Rules* to do so in the early stages of a relationship. Wait until he's visited you *three times* to visit him or meet him halfway – and even then, not too often.

Of course, some women will rationalize visiting a man first (or sooner than they should) by saying that they wanted to get away anyway – they haven't taken a holiday in years! Some reason that they have frequent flier miles so why not? Yes it would be fun and free, but it's not *The Rules*. Others convince themselves that the trip would be a great opportunity to visit a friend or relative. Please make sure you're not finding excuses to be in his city. If you do have a legitimate reason for being there – a business trip or your friend's hen party – don't tell him about it unless he specially asks if you're planning to be in his area anytime soon. If he does ask and you tell him your plans, don't let him assume you'll see him. He has to ask you out and come to your hotel or sister's home if he wants to see you.

If you travel to see him before he's made at least three trips to see you, he won't think you're special, hard to see, and will not appreciate you or pursue you in the future. Even if he was initially drawn to you, he will expect you to travel to him all the time. He might start calling you at the last minute for the weekend and saying that he's too busy to leave town and suggesting that you visit him again. He might even say he's too busy to pick you up at the airport. Soon he might say he's too busy to see you at all, even though you offered to visit him. Once you start breaking *The Rules*, even promising relationships start to unravel quickly.

We've heard from women who've met multimillionaires offering to send them plane tickets or even their private jets to bring them to their homes for the weekend as a first or second date. These women are naturally flattered and excited and think the offer is special and meaningful.

We tell them it may not be and to decline very sweetly. Even if he makes two million pounds a year and you're a struggling secretary, you must say, 'Thank you but I just can't get away this weekend.'

The reason is, he has to visit you. He has to work to see you – pack a suitcase, be inconvenienced, possibly miss the ballgame he was going to watch on TV. For a man to have his secretary call and make the arrangements requires no sweat on his part. For very little effort, he gets to have companionship and perhaps sex for the weekend. You have to get someone to watch your dog, experience jet lag, you have to stop your life and be inconvenienced. *Rules* girls don't turn themselves upside down for a good deal or fun weekend. They hold out for love and marriage!

So don't be blown away by a private plane, champagne and a limo. You might be the first woman he's met who ever said no. Don't worry. If he likes you, he'll visit you!

Assuming he is visiting you, what are *The Rules*?

For the first three times he visits you, he should not stay with you. If he asks to, say, 'I don't think so. We just met.' It will be up to him to find a place to stay – at a hotel or with a friend or relative. That's not your problem. Remember, the first three visits are really nothing more than three dates ... and on the first three dates we don't have sex with a man or have him stay at our place overnight. You can invite him on the third visit but he has to leave before the night is over. The fact that he's visiting from out-of-town doesn't change that.

Another reason not to let a man stay with you early on is to protect yourself from the type of guy who is more than happy to hop on a train or a plane to see you, but not for the reason you think. He's just looking to have a good time in a new city with a fun girl (you!) – nothing serious. You're just part of the trip, not the main attraction. By asking him to stay in a hotel, you'll have avoided this noncommittal, call-when-he's-coming-to-town type of relationship. You're not a hotel or a tourist attraction! Of course, there's nothing wrong with letting a man stay at your place as long as you can take it for what it is. But if you have dreams of love and romance, then you must do *The Rules*!

When he visits you the first three times, always see a little bit less of him than he would like. For example, if he suggests flying in Friday night and leaving Sunday evening, say Saturday morning would be better and end the weekend Sunday afternoon.

Don't cancel every single activity you normally do

on the weekend so that you can be with him every minute. For example, if you have a Saturday afternoon exercise class, go to it. Let him keep himself busy and wait for you.

The point is, don't be a woman who drops everything when a man is in town. You're a *Rules* girl ... you had a life before you met him and you still do! It's actually good for him if you have something – a previous commitment – other than him planned for that weekend. He should leave feeling that he didn't get enough of you instead of too much.

When he visits you, don't play social director. It's up to him to look into restaurants, museums, interesting places to take you or events going on that weekend. However, if he is not familiar with your town and asks you to suggest something to do, you can. But always err on the side of less. If he asks you to suggest a restaurant, do not pick out the romantic hot spot with the dim lighting and lovers' booths, but a decent place that you would take a friend or co-worker. Don't try too hard to find things to do so that he's entertained and not bored. Let him pick up the newspaper or an entertainment guide and figure something out, or make plans together when he arrives. Remember, he should think you were busy and just didn't have time to think about the weekend even if that's all you thought about all week.

Women have a tendency to think too much about the man, the weekend, and act on every thought. They make reservations at a Cajun restaurant because they remember he likes spicy food. They get two tickets to the auto show because he mentioned he was a car buff.

Your efforts might be noticed – but they'll backfire. He'll know you are intrigued and like him, that you remembered everything he ever said, and that you've been thinking about him all week and planning the perfect weekend. He'll feel smothered and you'll wonder why he stopped calling.

After he has visited you three times, you can visit him once and stay at his place, if he invites you. Who pays for the trip? It depends. If he offers to pay your travel costs, let him. If he doesn't, don't ask him for the money, but let him pay for everything when you're there. Don't worry. By doing *The Rules* – visiting him infrequently – you will automatically minimize your travel costs. On the other hand, do not visit him often just because he offers to pick up the tab. *The Rules* is about letting him pursue you, not saving money.

If you have friends or relatives in that city, it would be a good idea to call them and meet them briefly while you're there so that you don't spend the entire weekend with this man and he doesn't tire of you. End the weekend first.

Being in a long-distance relationship does not give you license to send men letters and greeting cards. You are not pen pals. You can send him a birthday or holiday card if you are in a committed long-distance relationship, assuming he sent you the same. The cards should be warm but not mushy. No love poetry.

If the relationship progresses – he's calling you every week for the weekend, he's visiting you more than you're visiting him, he wants to be exclusive and so on – you are in a long-distance *Rules* relationship. If this is not the case, be available to date others.

If things get serious, he might bring up the future and ask if you would ever consider relocating. Reply, 'I haven't really thought about it.' Until he actually proposes and gives you a ring, be vague. There is no reason to look into selling or renting your flat or asking for a job transfer to his city or finding a job in his city if he hasn't formally proposed.

In fact, there's no reason to relocate until after you've set a wedding date. We do not live with a man before marriage, and we don't go away with him on seven-day holidays before the honeymoon. Try to see him only on the weekends until you have a wedding date.

If you are already in a long-distance relationship and did not know about *The Rules* until now, start doing *The Rules* very strictly today. Don't call him. Let him call you. Get off the phone in fifteen minutes. (Okay, twenty minutes if he's calling from Tokyo or Paris and you don't talk that often!) If he's used to you travelling to him most of the time, let him visit you more now. If he says he's too busy, simply say, 'Things are so hectic ... I just can't get away right now.' This will get him to miss you, wonder about you, and figure out a way to visit you – if he's interested – and marry you!

Stop Dating Him If He Doesn't Buy You a Romantic Gift For Your Birthday or Valentine's Day

What kind of present can you expect to receive on your birthday when a man is in love with you? Ideally, jewellery, but any romantic gift will do. Now don't get us wrong. This is not a rule for gold diggers; it's just that when a man wants to marry you, he usually gives you jewellery, not sporty or practical gifts like a toaster or coffee maker. It is not how expensive the item is, but the *type* of gift it is. A typewriter can cost more than an inexpensive pair of earrings, and a computer, one would think, connotes love, being such a costly item; but such presents come from the head, not the heart, and are not good signs of love at all. Therefore, the *Rule* is that if you don't get jewellery or some other romantic gift on your birthday or other significant occasion, you might as well call it quits because he's not in love with you and chances are you won't get the most important gift of all: an engagement ring.

When men are in love, they give love objects even if they are on a tight budget. Flowers, jewellery, poetry and weekend trips to the country are the kinds of gifts given by men in love. Books, briefcases, toasters and other practical gifts are the kinds of things men give when they like you, care about you (like a sister), but don't really want to marry you.

Remember, gift giving has nothing to do with money. We know a poor student who could only afford a fifty pence greeting card for his girlfriend on Valentine's Day. He then spent four hours writing a beautiful love poem to her in it. A *Rules* present if there ever was one! As most women know, the time a man spends on anything is virtually priceless.

One more point about greeting cards: check to see if he signs 'love'. A man may sometimes send a greeting card with very casual intentions. If he doesn't sign it 'love', don't assume he does. When David was dating Claire, he signed his cards, 'Yours, David'. (I just *know* he loves me, she'd tell her friends.) They eventually had 'a talk' and he told her he wasn't in love with her. So don't assume anything. Just read what's written!

Furthermore, while a romantic gift is a must for birthdays, Valentine's Day and anniversaries, a man who is crazy about you will give you all kinds of things all the time. You're always on his mind, so you might get a stuffed animal he sees at a street fair or something kooky that's just perfect for you. For example, when Patty expressed an interest in biking, her boyfriend bought her a fancy helmet. If he didn't love her, he would have given her the helmet on her birthday, but being in love, he gave her a necklace and flowers on her birthday and the helmet to celebrate their six-month anniversary.

When you do receive gifts, don't overreact. When Suzi received roses from Kevin on their third date she was absolutely ecstatic. She rarely had been given flowers from anyone she liked, but she did *The Rules* things to do, she smiled, nonchalantly put them in vase, and said, 'Thank You!'

In general, *The Rule* is that when a man loves you he just wants to give you things. Anything. If your glass is empty in a restaurant, he wants to give you water or promptly asks the waiter to get it. If you can't see the screen in the cinema he asks five people to move over to give you another seat. If he sees you digging in your bag for a pen, he lends you his and then tells you to keep it. Basically, he notices everything about you, except anything bad. If you're ten pounds overweight, he doesn't think you're overweight, he thinks you're cute. But if your girlfriend (whom he is not in love with) is the same size, he thinks *she's* fat. When a man is not in love with you, he notices nothing or only the bad. For example, he might say, 'Lose weight and I'll take you on holiday.' You feel you have to earn his love. That's not *The Rules*, that's conditional love and not what we're after.

Again, this is not about being gold diggers or princesses wanting to be doted on all the time. It's about determining whether a man is truly in love with you and, if not, going on to the next. If you end up marrying a man who gives you a briefcase instead of a bracelet on your birthday, you may be doomed to a life of practical, loveless gifts and gestures from him such as food processors, and you may spend thousands of pounds in therapy trying to figure out why there's no romance in your marriage.

Don't Go Overboard and Other *Rules* for Giving to Men

As we explained earlier, you should not offer to pay for anything on the first three dates. There's no need to. When a man is interested in you, he is not thinking about money (i.e., splitting the bill), he's hoping to make a good impression and hoping that you'll see him again. Part of pursuing you is making plans and paying for everything.

Of course, if he *asks* you to split the bill, cheerfully do so. You weren't trying to get a free meal. You want him to *want* to pay for you. We don't tell a man to pick up the bill. We just notice he didn't and put it in the back of our mind. Maybe he's not Mr Right.

We are not telling you to be a gold digger. It is not about how much he spends. Let him take you to an inexpensive restaurant or a movie, as long as he plans ahead and pays for the date. When a man is truly in love, he'll work extra hours or borrow from his parents or friends to come up with the money to impress you. Dutch treat is fine for friends and co-workers, not dates. You want a man who is crazy about you!

Women, especially those making good salaries, tend to get hung up on reciprocating. We tell them that in the first two to three months of dating they should be focusing instead on getting off the phone first and not asking a man out – not obsessing about buying him dinner or a tie. When you're married, you can buy him anything you want!

After three months, you can make or buy him dinner.

On his birthday and/or other gift-giving holidays, *The Rules* are:

Do not spend more than thirty to seventy pounds, even if you can well afford to. But more importantly, don't buy him anything romantic.

Good gift ideas include:

1. A book on a subject of interest to him, as long as it has nothing to do with astrology, therapy, love or relationships, such as business, politics, computers or a novel (non-romantic) you know he'd love to read.
2. A winter scarf.
3. A T-shirt, sweatshirt or cap of his favourite sports team.

Do not buy him:

1. Jewellery
2. Anything monogrammed.
3. A picture frame or photo album.
4. Champagne glasses or any houseware for that matter.
5. A book of poems.

Women are not only too generous to men in material ways – they tend to be too extending in social situations as well. They invite a man they just started dating to accompany them to a wedding, dinner party, business or family function, country club, summer house or business trip/holiday. We strongly suggest you do not do so for at least three months. If you do, he will surely feel that you are more serious about the relationship than he is, get scared and pull back. In addition, if he is surrounded by married couples at these events, he will most surely feel pressured.

If you are in a business where you get free tickets to tennis matches, trips, or are regularly invited to business parties and shows as part of your job, do not take him for the first few months. Ask a friend or go alone. Why?

1. You will not be mysterious if he knows your entire social calendar.
2. He should not think of you as a cash cow. Otherwise, how will you know if he really cares about *you* or your perks? He must fall in love with you *first*!
3. When a man is in love with you, he wants to be with you. If you are always giving him presents and taking him to places, he might believe you are trying to buy his love and affection, that you are trying too hard and care too much, which is never good.

One more way a woman may try to give too much to a man is by being overly involved in his life. Needless to say, you can listen and offer suggestions, but don't become wrapped up in his business problems, family affairs or any other issues. You are not his therapist or his wife (yet).

Actually, the best gifts you can give a man is to do *The Rules*, which gives him the thrill of pursuing you and the glory of getting you!

Don't See Him More Than
Once or Twice a Week

Most men fall in love faster than women. They also fall out of love faster. They may want to see you two or three times a week, some even every day, in the beginning. If you give in and see them every time, eventually they get restless and irritable, and then stop calling. They seem moody a lot and say things like, 'I don't know what's wrong. I just have a lot going on right now.'

To keep a man from getting too much too soon, don't see him more than once or twice a week for the first month or two. Let him think you have 'other plans', that he is not the only man or interest in your life. When we hear someone say that she just met the greatest man and sees him every day, we think, 'Uh oh, this isn't going to turn out so well.' A woman *must* pace the relationship slowly. Don't expect a man to do it.

We know how painful this can be. It's only natural that when you meet a man you like who also likes you, you want to see him all the time. You want to know all about him – his favourite colour, his past relationships, what he eats for breakfast, everything – almost overnight. So it's hard for you to say no when he asks you out for Saturday night, Sunday brunch, and a

Monday night dinner and film all in one breath. But, girls, you must put your foot down! Don't make seeing you so easy. Men like sports and games – football, tennis, blackjack and poker – because they love a challenge. So be a challenge!

Remember, this *Rule* is not forever. After seeing him once a week for the first month, you can see him twice or three times a week during the second month, and three to four times a week in the third month. But never more than four or five times a week unless you're engaged. Men must be conditioned to feel that if they want to see you seven days a week they have to marry you. And until that blessed proposal occurs, you must practise saying no to extra dates even though you're dying to spend more time with him and even though you've mentally said to yourself, 'This is The One.'

If, for example, after kissing you passionately at the end of your first or second date he says, 'So what are you doing tomorrow?' summon up your sweetest voice and say, 'I'm sorry. I already have plans.' Stick to your ground, even if you feel intoxicated by the smell of his cologne on your neck. And, of course, don't say what your plans are or include him in them.

A man who is in love with you and hopes to marry you won't be put off by the once-to-twice-a-week dating structure you set up in the beginning. We find that only men who are just with you for fun or sex are likely to get angry or impatient. Don't be fooled if these men say the kinds of things that make you believe they want to marry you. It happens all the time. It's called Standard Operating Procedure.

On the first date, such a man might point to a restaurant and say, 'That's where my father proposed to my mother,' leading you to think that he will propose to you there one day. Or he might talk about the future, saying something like, 'In the summer we can go to the coast and I'll take you to this great seafood place.' You are naturally in heaven, thinking that this man has plotted out your lives forever. It might all be true and he may call again and ask you out. But it might be a ploy to get you into bed on the first or second date.

If you fall for his lines and see him every night that week — after all, you think he is serious about you — he might take you out a couple of times and have sex with you. But he may never call again or worse, he may continue to date you, but you'll end up watching his interest fade away. (A very painful thing. Watching someone falling 'out of love' is really awful!) If you follow *The Rules* and slow down the process, forcing him to get to know you and really fall in love, this will not happen.

The Rules will make you harder to get so that a man who doesn't really like you won't waste his or your time. So do yourself a favour and do *The Rules*. Don't see him more than once or twice a week!

No More Than Casual Kissing
on the First Date

It's common knowledge that men want as much as they can get on the first date. It's your job to slow them down. Let him kiss you on the first date, but nothing more. Keeping it to a kiss will force him not to think of you as just a physical object. If a *Rules* relationship is to develop, he must fall in love with your soul, your whole being, not just your body. So the less you do physically, the better. Besides, it's easier to stop something if you don't let things get too hot and heavy right away.

We know this is not an easy *Rule* to follow, particularly when you're out with someone really cute and he's driving fast in his sports car and kissing you at every red light. He's a great kisser and you wonder what else he's great at. This is when you have to brace yourself and say, 'The *Rule* is no more than casual kissing on the first date. No, don't invite him up to the flat. No, don't let his hands go everywhere.' If you're getting too excited, end the date quickly so you don't do anything you'll regret. If he wants more of you, let him call you and ask you for a second date.

Some men might make you feel that you're being old-fashioned or prudish. Some might make fun of you or even get angry. Let them know as nicely as you can that if they don't like it, they can get lost! If a man pressures you, then he's not someone you want to date. Keep telling yourself that other women have spoiled men by sleeping with them on the first date, but you're a *Rules* girl and you take your time. If he really cares about you, he will respect your boundaries. If he's a gentleman, he'll let the physical part of the relationship develop at your pace and never force anything on you. Forget all the 'free love' theories from the swinging sixties. Besides, it's not spontaneous or cool to have an unwanted pregnancy or a disease.

In addition, if you are following *Rule 10*: *How to Act on Dates 1, 2 and 3*, things should not get out of hand. As we said earlier, you should be talking about politics, books, good films, not marriage, kids, love, former boyfriends and girlfriends and sexual positions. The conversation should be cordial, not steamy, so you don't end up in bed after dessert. Besides, if you really like him, just kissing can be a lot of fun!

Don't Rush Into Sex and Other *Rules* for Intimacy

When is it okay to have sex? *The Rule* depends on your age and personal feelings. If you're eighteen and a virgin, you will want to wait until you are in a committed relationship. If you're thirty-nine, waiting a month or two can be fine. Of course, if you feel strongly against premarital sex, you should wait until you're married. If he loves you, he'll respect whatever decision you make.

But don't be surprised if the man you're dating gets very angry when you kiss him good night in the hall at the end of your second date rather than invite him up for a drink. He has probably been spoiled by other women who slept with him on the first or second date and now he feels he's being denied this pleasure. But don't worry. Anger indicates interest, and you might be surprised, for he will probably call you again!

But what if you like sex a lot too, and denying yourself is just as hard as denying him? Does that mean you sleep with him on the first or second date? Unfortunately, the answer is still no. You will just have to exercise a bit of self-restraint and character building here and trust that if you hold off for a few weeks or months, you won't be sorry. Why risk having him call you easy (and think of you that way) when he's talking to his mates in the locker room the next day? Better that he be angry and strategizing ways of seducing you on the next date than moving onto the next girl. Making him wait will only increase his desire and create more passion when you finally have sex whenever you're ready.

We know it can be excruciating to put sex off with someone you're attracted to, but you must think long-term here. If you play your cards right, you can have sex with him every night for the rest of your life when you're married!

Now you might argue that you don't mind having sex with him on the first or second date and taking your chances, that it's okay with you if he doesn't call again because you're both grown-ups and you can take your bumps. We know from experience, of course, that most girls who say this are lying to themselves. Deep down inside it's not okay with a woman if she sleeps with a man and he doesn't call. Every woman wants the man she just slept with to call her, that is, if she really likes him – and hopefully she likes the man she's sleeping with. Every woman we know who said it was okay if a man didn't call after sex was actually *not okay* when he didn't call. When you sleep with him on the second date, you don't really know if he's going to be gentleman or a creep. *Rules* girls don't take risks. We wait until we're sure before having sex.

Let's say that now, hopefully, you've held off for a

while and are ready to have sex with him. What *Rules* should you follow in bed? First and foremost, stay emotionally cool no matter how hot the sex gets. The fact is, most women turn men off not only because they sleep with them too soon, but because they talk too much about it in bed. They try to exploit the physical closeness of sex to gain emotional closeness, security and assurances about the future. The theories of Masters and Johnson (who are now divorced) are not to be ignored, but please wait a good amount of time before you begin holding lengthy seminars about your needs during sex or after sex. Don't be a drill sergeant, demanding that he do this or that. You have to trust that if you relax and let him explore your body like uncharted territory you will have fun and be satisfied. Being with you in bed should not be difficult or demanding. Don't bring anything – red light bulbs, scented candles, or X-rated videos – to enhance your sexual experience. If you have to use these things to get him excited, something's wrong. He should be excited about just sleeping with you.

While you're snuggling in bed after great sex is not the time to say, 'So, do you want me to make room in the wardrobe for your clothes?' or 'I put a toothbrush in the bathroom for you.' Don't bring up marriage, kids or your future together, not in bed (or out). Remember, these are *your* needs you are concerned about filling, and *The Rules* are a selfless way of living and handling a relationship. Men merely what to lie down next to someone they care about when they are feeling strong emotions.

Women are more curious, wanting to know, 'Now that we've slept together, where is this relationship going?' or 'What is the meaning of what we've just done?' While all these thoughts are whirling through your head and your desire to own this man is mounting from minute to minute, try to relax and think about nothing.

Don't cling to him if he has to leave that night or the following morning. Be casual and unmoved about the fact that the date is over. With that attitude, chances are he will be the one hanging on. Don't try to keep him there longer by suggesting brunch or sweet rolls and coffee in bed. If you do, he'll probably run to the nearest greasy spoon cafe for breakfast. Instead, go quietly about your business – brush your hair and teeth, do some sit-ups and stretches, brew coffee – and chances are he'll start massaging your shoulders and suggesting morning sex or a great brunch place.

It's only fair that if you're dating a man for a month or two and don't plan to sleep with him for a while to let him know. Otherwise, you're being a tease. On the other hand, what if you're more into sex than he is? *The Rules* answer is, if you don't want to feel insecure, then don't initiate sex. After you're in a committed relationship, when you know he is crazy about you, you can occasionally and playfully make an overture.

Last but not least, whenever you do have sex, always use a condom. Don't cave in when a man says, 'Just this once.' Remember, you're a *Rules* girl and you take good care of yourself.

Don't Tell Him What to Do

If your boyfriend wants to join the new 'in' health club where all the leggy model types work out, don't tell him to jog on the street or exercise at home. Say, 'That's great!' and go about your business. Don't show that you are jealous or insecure. If he loves you, it won't matter how pretty the girls at the gym are.

If he'd rather go camping with his friends on the weekends than be with you, either let him or break up with him, but don't tell him what to do. Our friend Daisy was seeing Joe for a couple of months when he suddenly started to make weekend plans with his friends. Conditioned by her therapist to be honest and up front about her feelings, Daisy told Joe that she felt abandoned. He immediately started making weekend plans with her. She was ecstatic. But after a month of togetherness, he suddenly stopped calling. She never heard from him again.

The moral of the story: don't play social director. If Joe didn't want to spend weekends with Daisy, being asked to wasn't going to change his mind. Men do what they want to do. If they can't live without you, it's very clear. If they can live without you, it's also clear. Don't be dense. Read the tea leaves and move on to the next man if necessary!

If, after dating you for months, he has never introduced you to his parents or friends, that means he doesn't want you to meet his parents or friends. He may simply be shy about the whole thing. Don't be pushy and suggest meeting them if he doesn't bring it up. We don't force ourselves on the family. We don't make friends with his roommate or take his mother to lunch so that she'll tell him to marry us. No one can make him marry us. Either accept the situation as it is and be patient, or date others, but don't force anything to happen.

Finally, don't try to change his life in any way. Don't go through his cupboards and throw out his favourite but disgusting old jeans and then suggest you and he go shopping for new ones. Don't try to turn him on to tennis when he loves drinking beer and watching football. Don't sign him up for career counselling courses because *you're* unhappy with his current job. Don't push your interests on him either. If he loves steak, don't preach the virtues of vegetarianism. You don't own him. Don't fix him. You will end up emasculating him and he will come to see you as a domineering shrew. He wants someone who makes him feel good or better, not inadequate. So leave him alone. When he *asks* you what to wear or how to play tennis, you can help him. Until then, just be there.

Let Him Take The Lead

Dating is like slow dancing. The man must take the lead or you fall over your feet. He should be the first one to say 'I love you,' 'I miss you,' 'I've told my parents so much about you. They can't wait to meet you.'

He should be an open book, you should be a mystery. Don't tell him he's the first person you've felt this way about in a long time, or that you never thought you'd fall in love again.

Remember, let him take the lead. He declares love first, just as he picks most of the films, the restaurants and the concerts the two of you go to. He might some-times ask you for your preference, in which case you can tell him.

You should meet his parents before he meets yours unless, of course, he picks you up at your parents' house. Let your mother or father open the door, but don't let them hang around too much. Tell your mother not to smile at him as if he were her son-in-law and don't let her mention your sister's upcoming wedding. Remember, mothers can get quite anxious about your dating life. So be ready to go when he arrives – don't be in the bathroom applying more mascara – so that your parents don't spend too much time with him alone, asking him questions like, 'How's business?' or 'So what are your intentions?'

The same rule applies to your friends. He should introduce you to his friends before you introduce him to yours. You should double with his married or dating friends before you double with yours.

Reciprocate when you feel quite secure about the way the relationship is going and don't tell your friends too much about him because they might inadvertently blab when they do meet him. If you can't trust them to be quiet and discreet, then say nothing. The last thing you need is a well-meaning, but not too clever friend, saying something like, 'Oh, it's nice to meet you. Sheila has told me *so* much about you'.

Don't worry. After he proposes, he will eventually meet all your friends and family. Until then, just follow his lead!

Don't Expect a Man to Change
or Try to Change Him

Let's say you have met the man of your dreams – almost. There are a couple of things you wish were different. What do you do? Nothing! Don't try to change him because men never *really* change. You should either accept certain flaws or find someone else. Of course, it all depends on what it is about him that bothers you.

If he is fanatically neat, chronically tardy, hates Chinese food (your favourite) and disco dancing (you love it), or he won't part with his childhood cigarette card collection, but he loves you to death, consider yourself lucky. These are annoying but relatively harmless vices, which we classify under category A.

On the other hand, if he flirts with other women in front of you at parties, exhibits violent behaviour at times, pays no attention when you are telling him something important, or forgets your birthday, then he is into category B (bad) behaviour and you have some heavy-duty thinking to do.

In the case of A, pray for acceptance and don't nag him. It won't work anyway. Just be ready at 9 p.m. when he says he'll be over at 8.

When it comes to B-type behaviour, such as infidelity and lack of consideration, seriously think about ending the relationship. People don't change that much and you can't *count* on it happening. What you see is what you get. If a man cheated on you during your courtship, he may do so during your marriage. He might be on his best behaviour for a while after you catch him the first time. But don't delude yourself. Old habits die hard.

You must decide if you can live with him. Whether or not he ever cheats on you again, realize that the thought will always cross your mind. You might find yourself checking his shirt collar for lipstick stains and his pockets for little pieces of paper with women's phone numbers on them, or calling him at the office when he says he's working late. Is that how you want to live? If it is, *Rules* women make up their minds and live with it. The key to a successful marriage is to be happy with the way things are, not the way they could be *if only* he changed.

Of course, a playboy type who falls in love with you because you did *The Rules* will automatically mend his ways. He will want to be monogamous because you, unlike other women he's dated, are busy, don't call him, make him wait for sex and don't bring up marriage or the future. Therefore, his object in life is to win you over. He has very little interest in other women because he has no time for them! Thoughts of how to conquer you consume most of his waking hours. You have become the biggest challenge in his life. Do *The Rules* and even the biggest playboy can be all yours!

Deciding whether or not you can live with a man's bad habits or his past (ex-wives and children) is not easy. Also, some character traits don't fall so easily into either category A or B. For example, your man may be someone who doesn't live up to his earning potential. Whether you can live with him depends on how important money, career, status and a big house are to you.

In all such cases, you must sit quietly with yourself and ask for guidance to do the right thing. Consulting others helps, but remember you have to live with these things yourself. Ask yourself if you can really marry an ex-womaniser or a recovering alcoholic. Can you really live with the possibility that he may cheat or drink again? Ask yourself if you can live with stepchildren or past infidelity. If the answer is yes, great. But if you are too troubled by his past or current behaviour, you might have to do *The Rules* thing and walk away. Taking him to couples therapy in the hopes of changing him can take forever, rarely works, and some things just cannot be changed.

Whatever you do, don't nag him or he's sure to resent you for it. So think long and hard, but don't waste too much time deciding. Remember, there are lots of men out there!

Don't Open Up Too Fast

Dating is not therapy. There are many ways to kill a relationship. Getting heavy and examining everything is certainly one of them. Conditioned by self-help books to tell all, women tend to overdo it on first dates, bringing up past relationships, their hurts and fears, their alcohol or drug problem – all in an attempt to bond with this new man. This is deadly and boring. Be intelligent but light, interesting yet mysterious. That's why we have suggested not opening up too fast. (See also *Rule 10: How to Act on Dates 1, 2 and 3.*) The first date should be short, so you don't say too much. Remember, the person who talks the most has the most to lose.

By the end of the first date, he should know just a few facts, such as your name, your profession, how many siblings you have, where you went to college, where you grew up, and your favourite restaurants. By the end of the first date, he should not know your dating history. Don't reprimand him for picking you up thirty minutes late and then tell him you were afraid he would never show up, that you felt abandoned, and explain that 'abandonment' is one of your issues in therapy. Don't tell him that his behaviour reminds you of your ex-boyfriend who was also never on time. Even if this is true, don't tell him. Don't worry. By doing *The Rules*, you will automatically attract a loving, attentive husband who will be around so much that you won't have time to think about your abandonment issues!

If you have a burning desire to tell him a secret, *The Rules* credo is 'Haste makes waste.' It's always better to wait before telling someone something that you might feel ashamed or nervous about. Wait at least a couple of months. Better yet, wait until after he says 'I love you.' Unless he loves you, it's none of his business anyway!

Too many women tell intimate details of their lives far too soon. This is not only unwise, it doesn't work. No man wants to be the recipient of a therapy session upon first meeting you. No man wants to hear how messed up your life has been before he *really* loves you.

You are not on this date to get sympathy but to have a nice evening and get him to call you again. Remember *Rule 10* – that the first three dates are about being light and charming, like a summer breeze. Men must always remember you as mysterious on the first three dates. Their initial impression tends to go a long way. If and when things get serious, you can casually tell him about your difficult childhood and some of your fears. Even then, tell him in an easy, short, simple way. Don't be dramatic about your past. Don't go into long details. Don't be burdensome.

Let's say you are a recovering alcoholic. He takes you out for a drink on your first date and to dinner on the second. He notices you only ordered club soda both times. He is about to order a bottle of wine and wants to know if you'll join him. Don't say, 'No, I *never* drink. I hit a terrible bottom with drugs and alcohol two years ago and now I'm sober in AA.' Just say, 'No, thanks,' and smile. After a couple of months when he's madly in love with you and you feel that he would not judge you for your drinking problem, you can tell him something like, 'I used to drink a lot in college. It really made me sick. Now I'm in AA and I don't drink anymore. I feel better.' Then smile and go on to other, more pleasant conversation. If he loves you, he will not make you feel bad. He won't argue with you or try to encourage you to 'just have one.' He might even start drinking less himself to make you feel better. He might even say that he's proud of your sobriety and discipline.

If you've had a serious illness and you're embarrassed about obvious scars from your surgery, wait until you're about to be intimate with him and then casually mention, as you take your clothes off in the dark, that you had an illness. If he loves you, he will kiss and caress you. Don't bring up the illness in a serious, heart-to-heart talk on your first date. Remember, especially in the beginning, don't be too intense about anything or lay all your cards on the table. In general, the less tragic you are about your life circumstances, the more sympathy you will probably get. Ask for sympathy and you never get it.

If you don't know how to hold on to money, don't balance your cheque book, have an answering machine filled with calls from debt collectors, don't tell him what a mess you are with finances and that you got it from your gambling father. Now you might feel that we are asking you to act casually about your problems, but the fact is, you are bad with money and he will soon see that. But does he really have to know about the creditors and your cancelled credit cards? No, all he has to know is that money is not your strong suit.

We are not suggesting that you hide or lie about bad things in your life, just that you not burden him with all the gory details too soon. Does he really have to know that your last boyfriend dropped you for your best friend? Can't you just say, if he asks, that your last relationship 'just didn't work out'?

He should always feel that he's in love with the girl of his dreams, not someone damaged. If you *feel* damaged read *Rule 1* again and again. Remember, you are a creature unlike any other! It's when and how you tell him your dark secrets, not the secrets themselves, that matter.

By the time you are engaged, he should know all that really matters about you and your family and your past. *The Rules* are truthful and spiritual in nature. It is morally wrong to accept an engagement ring without revealing whatever truths about yourself you need to share. Tell him these things in a calm, non-dramatic manner and don't, as some women do, surprise him with these skeletons after you're married. That's not the time to tell him that you were previously married or never finished college. It's not fair to him and not good for a *Rules* marriage.

Be Honest But Mysterious

Men love mystery! Fifty years ago it was easier to be mysterious with men. Women lived at home and their mothers answered the phone and never told the men who else called their daughters. Dates didn't see women's bedrooms so soon. Today, men pick up women at their flats, see their lingerie in the bathroom, their romance novels in the living room, and hear their phone messages. While such openness is good for marriage, it's important to project a certain amount of mystery during the dating period.

We are all looking for someone to share our lives, thoughts and feelings with, but as we suggested in *Rule 24* wait until he says he loves you to share your innermost secrets. When he is in your home don't listen to your answering machine. Let him wonder who called besides him! You might know that the messages are probably from girlfriends feeling suicidal about their dating situations, but he doesn't!

If your date is at your place and one of your friends calls, don't say, '*Eddie's* over. I can't talk'. That means you've been talking about Eddie to your friends and he's somehow important. Even if that is the case, Eddie should not know that he is the subject of your thoughts and conversations or he might think he doesn't have to work so hard to get you. Simply say, 'I can't talk right now. I'll call you later'. After you hang up, don't tell him who called or why.

Before he comes to your home, tuck this book away and make sure any self-help books are out of sight. Have interesting or popular novels or non-fiction books in full view. Hide in the closet anything you don't want him to see, such as a bottle of Prozac.

In general, don't give away any information that is not absolutely necessary. If you are busy on the night he asks you for a date, don't tell him what you're planning to do. Just say you are busy. If he asks you out for the weekend, don't say, 'I'm visiting my brother this weekend. His wife just had a baby.' Simply say, 'I'm sorry, but I already have plans.' Less is more. Let him wonder what you are doing. You don't have to be an open book. This is good for him and it's good for you. It keeps the intrigue going. You don't want to make dating you so easy and predictable that he loses interest. Always remember that in time you will be able to tell him just about anything!

On the other hand, *Rules* girls don't lie either. Don't tell a Mel Gibson-type guy that you love hiking when you can't stand trees, insects and backpacks. And certainly don't tell your boyfriend that you love and want children because he does when you really don't. Take our advice. Don't lie. It's a law of the universe.

Don't Live With a Man
(or Leave Your Things in His House)

To live together or not to live together? Is that a question you're grappling with now? Your friends (not knowing *The Rules*) might say, 'Do it'. Your parents (being conservative) will no doubt say, 'No'. *The Rules* answer is: 'Move in only if you've set a wedding date.' In other words, the only reason to live with someone is if you're planning the wedding and you don't want to pay two rents.

Contrary to popular belief, living together is not a trial period for him to see how he feels about you. He either loves you or he doesn't, and playing house and cooking him a lot of breakfasts won't change a thing. In fact, sometimes, the best way for him to see how he feels about you is to not see you at all. You may have to dump him if he can't commit. If he really loves you, he'll beg you to come back. If he doesn't, you've lost nothing, saved time and can now go on to someone else.

Women who think that commitment will come *after* they shack up often learn the hard way that this is not the case. Of course, by the time the lesson is learned, their self-esteem is shattered and they're two or three or four years older. Does this scenario sound familiar?

After dating James for a year and a half, Wendy wanted a ring. James wouldn't budge. They decided to live together to see if they could 'work it out' (his idea and word choice). Nothing changed. When he went away on business trips he didn't call or think about her that much. Nine months and a lot of wasted time later, he was still not in love and so he moved out. Wendy attributed the break-up to his parents' messy divorce. The truth is, she should have just ended it sooner when he wouldn't commit.

If you operate under the delusion that living together without a real commitment will somehow bring you closer together, you should know that many women tell us that their husbands proposed after they *moved away from, not toward*, the relationship. One women booked a trip to Club Med with a girlfriend after dating her boyfriend for a year, another started getting very busy and unavailable on weekends, and a third talked about taking a job in another city. Then, their husbands proposed.

Remember, men don't necessarily propose when you're cuddled up on the couch watching a rented video, but do so when they're afraid of losing you. In *Love Story* – a movie you should study like the Bible – Oliver proposes to Jenny (a *Rules* girl, if there ever was one) after she says she's planning to take a scholarship in France and after suggesting that their opposite (rich/poor) backgrounds would not mix well. Jenny wasn't grateful or loving at that moment – she almost broke off their relationship. (You don't have to go that far!) But be a little distant and difficult. The unobtainable is always more exciting; men very often want something more just because they can't have it.

If you are following *The Rules* (particularly *Rule 18: Don't See Him More than Once or Twice a Week*), you can't possibly live with him, by design or by accident. Women who tell us that they moved in with a man accidentally, as a result of spending long weekends with him, obviously broke a few rules along the way. You stay over a lot and one thing leads to another. First you get a drawer, then a shelf, and then a wardrobe of your own. Before you or he realize it, you're having your post delivered to his flat and your friends are leaving messages on his tape machine.

Needless to say, this should not be happening. If you are doing *The Rules*, you never need a wardrobe full of clothes and accessories at his place. Don't leave your toothbrush or bathrobe there. He should be begging you to leave things in his apartment and going out of his way to make shelf space. This invasion of space should not come from you. You are independent, you are not a crasher, you are always ending the evening (or the morning) first. (Besides, the less he sees of some of your less glamorous habits, like the way you floss your teeth or the sound you make when you slurp your coffee, the better).

Is there any reason to live with a man if you haven't set a wedding date? Yes, and that's when he wants to and you don't! He's crazy about you and you're not so sure about him. In this case, he's taking the risk, not you. Still, proceed with caution. Living with him may prevent you from dating others and meeting someone you're crazy about, so how smart is it?

Observe His Behaviour on the Holidays

How he treats you on holidays is a good barometer of how he feels about you!

When a man is in love, he thinks about you and makes special plans with you *in advance* of Valentine's Day, New Year's Eve, your birthday and Christmas or its equivalent. He'll circle the dates on his calendar and try to get the best table at a romantic restaurant – and that could mean calling a week or two ahead of time!

If it's Valentine's Day, he'll call the florist and buy you roses or your favourite flowers. If it's your birthday, he might buy you a piece of jewellery and a meaningful card. He might suggest you spend the holidays with his family and make sure you see in the New Year together in a romantic way. He'll make a thoughtful toast about the two of you. You're always on his mind and in his heart.

He looks forward to being with you on that special night and watching you read his card and open his present. What should you give him? A *Rules* girl gives a man she is dating *a simple card* for Valentine's Day – something short and sweet; no poetry and no balloons – and maybe a scarf or sweater for his birthday or the holidays. (See *Rule 17: Don't Go Overboard and Other Rules for Giving to Men.*)

When a man is not in love, he sometimes doesn't even acknowledge the holidays. He may take you out on Saturday night as he normally does and not even mention the holiday – even if it falls on the next day – hoping that you don't either. You may blame his lack of romantic interest in you at holiday time on his upbringing or past relationships, but a man in love with a woman acts differently with her than with anyone else.

If he's really not planning to marry you, he may not even call you the week of Valentine's Day or New Year's Eve. He may skip the week to avoid the whole issue. If you ask him why he didn't call, he might say things were hectic at work or holidays are silly. But a man in love would not be too busy or cynical about the holidays. In fact, we've known a few men who even carved pumpkins for their girlfriends on Halloween, hardly an important occasion.

When a man is not in love, he may buy a silly card and just sign his name – with no 'love'. He finds the holidays stupid or commercial and gets irritable if you take it seriously or expect more from him.

If the man you are dating does little or nothing for your birthday, Valentine's Day, or New Year's Eve, what should you do?

Don't bring up the occasion either. Pretend you forgot or didn't care – and then cry to your girlfriends. Just don't let him know it bothered you!

Don't have a 'talk' about how you thought your first

Valentine's Day or birthday together would be more romantic and are really disappointed and hurt. You can't make a man feel romantic if he doesn't. If these special occasions are not important to him you must accept this.

Don't hint that it's Valentine's Day or pressure him to take you out or buy you flowers. He either thought of it and wanted to or he didn't. Don't try to get something from the wrong source. Buy yourself flowers if that's important to you.

If you demand that he takes you out to buy you flowers, he may comply, but it won't be from his heart. He may do it just to avoid an argument or to continue to see you (until he meets someone else) or to have sex. It never works *long-term* if we force things.

If the man you are dating did not ask you out on New Year's Eve or Valentine's Day or did not suggest spending Christmas together, you cannot ask him to. Man must pursue woman! Do not offer to make him a candlelit dinner at your place (to make it easy for him or so that he doesn't have to plan or spend money). If he didn't initiate a romantic evening with you, then he didn't want to be romantic with you. Just put it in the back of your head that this man is not romantic or not in love with you and either accept that or move on. This a good time to re-evaluate the relationship and determine if he is your Mr Right.

On Valentine's Days and New Year's Eves in the past – before you discovered *The Rules* – you may have overlooked signs that a man wasn't in love with you.

You may have rationalized his no card/silly card, and told yourself these gestures were not important. But in your heart, you knew the truth. You knew that a man in love would have bought you flowers or tried to do something special.

Now that you know *The Rules*, what do you do that night if the man you are dating did not ask you out at least several days – preferably a week – in advance for an important occasion?

Make plans with your friends or go to a party where you might meet someone else. The holidays can be a very lonely and painful time for a single woman, so try not to be home by yourself.

But even if all you do is stay at home, make sure to leave your answering machine on so, in case he calls, he doesn't know where you are. It really doesn't matter what you do that night as long as you don't – in a weak moment – call him and invite him over. Rent a video or invite a girlfriend over for dinner, and think seriously about breaking up with this guy. Resolve to do *The Rules* on every man you meet from this moment so you don't spend your next birthday/Valentine's Day/New Year's Eve/Christmas or holiday alone!

Rules for Personal Ads and Dating Services

If you are planning to use personal ads, voice-mail ads, video dating, or matchmaking services to meet men, we recommend that you place the ad and let men respond to you.

Why? It goes back to the basic premise of *The Rules*: man pursues woman. He must search through a sea of print ads, voice mails, or video images and pick *yours* out. He has to like *your* hair colour, *your* distinctive voice, the way your wrote *your* ad, *your* height and profession, and so on. Remember, he's the hunter! Every man has a type, a voice or a look he likes. There has to be a spark for him that attracts him to you, something that makes him find you unexplainably special.

We have found that responding to a man's ad doesn't seem to work as well. Answering his ad, liking his type, liking his voice or looks or what he does for living puts you in the unwanted position of being the pursuer. In addition, he'll know you are interested in him or his type and the challenge will be over.

Of course, even if he picks you out and likes you, there's no guarantee that you'll like him. But this would also be true at a bar or a party. You wouldn't go up to

117

the guy who's 'your type'; but you would wait for a man to approach you. The same pretty much applies to dating services and ads, although it's not quite as black and white.

You just need to keep going on dates until a man who responds to your ad is someone who appeals to you. Hopefully, you are getting lots of responses from men – see the tips below for placing an ad that draws the most letters – and have many choices. Having many men to choose from is always good – the more dates you have, the more practice you will get, and you will be less inclined to get hung up on any particular man.

What should your ad say?

To get the most and best responses, your ad should be short, light, flirtatious and focused on your physical attributes, not your feelings. If you are placing a print or voice-mail ad, you must give him a mental picture of you.

You may find it difficult to describe your appearance. If so, one method we've found to be effective is to say which model or actress or well-known personality you resemble. Don't lie, but don't be modest either. Hasn't anyone ever told you you look like someone famous? If you're tall, blond and slim, try to think of a well-known model with those attributes. If you are short with dark hair and big eyes, perhaps there's a movie star or TV sitcom character you resemble. Ask your friends to help you come up with someone who you could honestly say you look like. Put it in your ad. Men love this stuff!

Limit your ad to about four lines and stick to the facts – age, height, profession and hobbies. Don't say you're looking for true love or romance. He should think you're just dating.

Here's a good voice-mail ad:

'I am twenty-eight years old, five feet seven inches with long brown straight hair and green eyes. People tell me I look like (model/movie star). I'm a dental hygienist. I like tennis and swimming. Well, that's me! [Giggle] Have a great day.'

Here's an ad you would *not* want to use, even if this is exactly how you feel:

'At the end of my rope. It's really hard to meet men so I decided to try this. I'm thirty-five, a financial analyst, looking for someone to spend the rest of my life with. I'm not into playing games.'

Aside from the fact that a man seeing or hearing this has no idea what she looks like, the ad is much too serious, too revealing and quite depressing.

When you receive responses, call the men you are interested in meeting when you think they will not be home and leave your name and phone number on their answering machine. Of course, if he answers, only stay on the phone for ten minutes.

Assuming you get his machine and he calls you back, still don't stay on the phone for more than ten minutes. Hopefully he will set up a date to meet you within that period of time. If not, hang up after ten minutes anyway. Staying on the phone longer to give him more time to ask you out is not *The Rules*. Don't become best friends on the phone. We know women who stayed on the phone for hours getting to know men who answered their ads. These men never even asked to meet them or they made tentative plans and then didn't follow through. They proved to be complicated or unreliable. In cases where a relationship did start, it usually fizzled within a few months. There was no mystery, no build-up – it was simply too much too soon. This won't happen if you're getting off the phone in ten minutes. Get to know him on dates.

So if you don't have many blind dates and you haven't connected recently with any men at singles events, work or the gym, you should most definitely try personal ads and dating services. The men who respond to ads and sign up with services are usually serious about meeting someone and often marriage-minded – otherwise, why would they spend the time or money? In fact, we know several women who met and married men through ads and dating services.

In conclusion, our advice is to try everything until you meet Mr Right! Remember, placing an ad or joining a dating service does not mean you should stop going to parties, bars, resorts, singles weekends, or taking up a social sport like tennis. The bottom line is: Never give up and never stop trying!

Rules for On-Line Dating

Dating on the Internet has become incredibly popular in recent years. So what do we think of on-line dating? To be perfectly honest, while we encourage you to try it if you haven't been able to meet men any other way, we have found that these relationships usually don't pan out. At best, women end up with male friends or pen pals, not husbands.

The main problem with on-line dating is that the relationships are based on chatting – not physical attraction, the spark so necessary for a *Rules* relationship.

In addition, on-line dating can be downright *dangerous*. You have probably read articles about women raped or killed by men they met through the Internet. The truth is, no matter how nice, interesting or sincere the person seems to be on-line, all you know about him is what he tells you. He could be a lunatic, a rapist, a killer, a teenager having fun or a married man – you just don't know!

Of course, we understand why some women prefer dating on the Internet to the singles scene. They are fed up with searching for Mr Right at bars and parties. If they don't feel attractive, they think they are at a disadvantage in social situations. They believe that they have a better chance of attracting a man with their mind, great personality or witty way of writing, than their looks. The Internet allows them to date with no make-up on and in sweatpants.

We understand how they feel, but we just don't think this method works as well as face-to-face meetings. The best romantic relationships start out with physical chemistry. Internet relationships are based on chatting. We know several women who spent months talking to men on the Internet before meeting them. Few of these relationships worked out. He calls you his 'soul mate', the one who knows his innermost thoughts and dreams and then marries someone else he's really attracted to!

But if you are determined to meet men on-line, we suggest that you do *The Rules* the best you can so you don't waste time conversing with men who will never marry you or put yourself in danger. Here are some suggestions:

1. Once he's shown interest in you – responded to your personal ad or approached you in a chat room – tell him you'd like to exchange photos by E-mail right away. There's no point in continuing an on-line romance if he's not attracted to you.

2. Once he's seen your photo, it's up to him to suggest meeting you. (If he doesn't, then he's not crazy about your looks and it's *next*!) If he lives in another city, he should visit your city. You don't visit him. (See *Rules 14 & 15: Rules for long-distance*

relationships).We've heard about women who 'hop on a train' to meet a man they've been chatting with for weeks or months. *Rules* girls let men visit them! When he hops on a train or drives to visit you, you must meet at a public place. *He should not know where you live!*

We cannot stress the safety factor enough. We've heard about women who risked their lives because they invited men they met on-line to their home on the first or second date. This is dangerous. In addition, make sure to give a friend or relative any information about the date – who, what, where, when – so he or she can keep track of your whereabouts.

3. Don't use the Internet to have heart-to-heart conversations or to bond with a man. Many women think that *The Rules* – i.e., don't open up too fast, be honest but mysterious – don't apply to on-line dating. They wonder how they can get to know this stranger if they don't tell him their whole life story right away. They think nothing of baring their souls or discussing their past relationships and their desire to meet and marry Mr. Right. And if he lives in another city and they don't see him that often, they feel that justifies frequent E-mails.

Don't kid yourself. E-mails are no different from phone calls, letters and greeting cards. We don't call men, we don't write them letters or cards and we don't overdo E-mail.

Whether you are dating on-line or face-to-face, men are still men. They do not fall in love with and marry the women who send them the most revealing and most frequent E-mails, even if they say that's what they want. They might tell you that they like women who are honest and open, who say they want a commitment if they want a commitment, who don't play games. But they actually chase and/or marry women they are physically attracted to, who are elusive and challenging and whose E-mails are as well. Short and sweet is always the best.

If you're on the computer chatting with him so much, how challenging are you? How interesting can your life be if you are glued to your terminal and have time to chat with him ten times a day?

Let him get into the habit of E-mailing you interesting titbits about his day without necessarily receiving a response every time. Remember, on-line or in person, you are a creature unlike any other and worth pursuing, so let him.

Don't Waste Time on Fantasy Relationships

If you have a good rapport with your doctor, lawyer or accountant, you may find yourself wondering if he's interested in you romantically. You're not alone, but you may not be seeing the situation for what it is. How can you know for sure? It's simple. Has he ever asked you out? Has he ever suggested having a drink, lunch or dinner? If the answer is no, then he's not!

This may sound obvious, but you'd be surprised how many women tell themselves it's romance when a man pays them the slightest attention out of professional courtesy. Unless he asks to spend time with you in a non-professional capacity, a relationship beyond business does not exist – and *Rules* girls don't waste their time on non-existent relationships!

The fact is, when a man is interested in a woman – including a female patient or client, employer or employee – he finds some way to ask her out. He may invite her to work out at his gym, attend a fund-raiser with him or play tennis over the weekend. He may not necessarily ask her out for a Saturday night date since that might be too obvious, or awkward, or forward, but he'll figure out some way to see her outside of the office.

This behaviour is different from the professional courtesy of a physician or financial advisor, who might say, 'Call me anytime,' which women mistakenly interpret as romantic interest.

Let's examine three fantasy relationships and *The Rules*'s answers to remove any doubt you might have about a similar situation in your life.

Fantasy Relationships #1: Your internist of two years told you 'beep me anytime' if your asthma acts up. He once told you to call him by his first name. He puts his arm around your shoulders when he escorts you out of his office. You just know he would ask you out if you weren't his patient. And, naturally, you want to have a 'talk' with him or ask him out!

The Rules answer: If a doctor is friendly, affectionate, concerned and kind, then he's doing his job. It's not a come-on for a doctor to tell a patient to beep him or call the office 'day or night' if his patient has asthma — people can die of asthma and it's his job to make sure his patients stay alive and well. Some doctors are informal (it's okay to call them by their first name) and others are touchy-feely (they kiss *all* their patients hello and goodbye). It's just good bedside manners — and good business — for a doctor to show warmth and caring. If he were romantically interested in you and uncomfortable about dating a patient, he would refer you to his associate and then ask you out.

Sure, it's a little more complicated for a doctor, lawyer or CEO to pursue a patient, client or associate.

But it's not impossible. We've heard about bosses who've dated and even married their employees, even though it was frowned upon by the company. At first they kept the relationship a secret and then they voluntarily decided he or she would transfer to another division or another company so they could date freely.

Fantasy Relationship #2: Your accountant called you over the weekend to remind you to send in your tax forms before April 15. You think because he called you on Saturday at home instead of during the week at work there might be something there.

The Rules answer: Accountants work on the weekends, especially during the busy tax season. The lines between work and home, during-the-week and weekends can be very blurry in business. Unless he suggested brunch, don't read into it.

Fantasy Relationship #3: You think the waiter at the restaurant you go to twice a week likes you because he always remembers how you like your eggs and that you take your coffee light with two sugars. You think he's more attentive to you than other customers — refills your coffee before you ask — and always make conversation with you. You want to let him know you're not seeing anyone seriously and would go out with him if he asked. The problem is, he hasn't. What to do?

The Rules answer: Waiters are in the service business. It's normal for a waiter to remember a regular customer's preferences. He works for tips so it's in his interest to be friendly, make conversation, get your order right. If he liked you beyond this, however, he would suggest having drinks one night.

The point bears repeating: When a man is really interested in a woman, he figures out some way to ask her out.

Don't be insulted. We're not suggesting that your doctor, broker or accountant isn't fond of you, just that it's not a *Rules* relationship until he asks you out.

Also keep in mind that many men, including professionals, like to flirt with women. Looking at lab results, contracts and financial statements all day can get pretty boring, so it's fun for them to make small talk, notice your figure if you're in good shape and compliment you on your new hairstyle. After all, they are men and they do like to look at women! It's also an ego boost for them to put on the charm, knowing that it gives some of their female patients/clients high school girl crushes. But it's all quite harmless, so don't take it seriously unless he asks you on a date.

We're not saying that you can't daydream about your sexy doctor or look forward to quarterly meetings with your handsome financial planner. Being a *Rules* girl doesn't mean you can't have obsessions, it means you don't act on them.

The danger lies in thinking there's a relationship there and not being open to real relationships. Women who are absorbed in fantasy relationships usually don't have real ones!

Ask yourself, are you doing everything to meet men

or are you living for the day when your dream lover asks you out? You're less likely to place a personal ad, sign up with a dating service or take that singles ski trip if you believe you're in a relationship.

Remember, *Rules* girls know they're either dating a man or not. There's nothing in between.

So if you thought your broker or lawyer was interested in you, but now you realize he may like you but not romantically, try to accept the truth instead of fighting it. Your first impulse may be to clear the air, be open and honest – ask him if he has feelings for you but isn't acting on them because of your professional relationship. You might want to write him a note or, worse, a long letter explaining how you feel.

Don't. First, that's not *The Rules*. He must initiate any such talk. Second, nothing good will come of it. If you talk to him and he tells you that you misread his politeness and that he's just as nice to every other client/patient, you'll feel foolish and hurt – not to mention embarrassed about seeing him again professionally.

If, on the other hand, he tells you he is attracted to you, but has decided not to pursue the relationship because he's involved with someone else or more interested in you as a client/patient than a lover, you're not much better off. You have the ego satisfaction of knowing that he's attracted to you, but so what? You still don't have a Saturday night date, much less a relationship. And it's a hollow victory anyway because if he was really *crazy* about you – and why would a *Rules* girl settle for anything less? – he would rather date you than just have a professional relationship with you.

So if you can't tell him how you feel, what can you do?

The Rules. Look your best whenever you see him, end all phone calls/meetings first, show no interest in him personally, don't send him holiday cards (if you mistakenly thought that would make him think about you in a different light) or invite him to your New Year's party to pave the way from a professional relationship to a social one. Don't buy him a tie for Christmas or bake him cookies for the holidays. Gifts don't make men think about women or ask them out. Try to treat him as you would an elderly or unattractive man – not the handsome hunk you think he is! – someone you wouldn't think twice about, much less bake brownies for!

Doing *The Rules* won't make him ask you out if he was never going to, but it will keep you from wasting time baking cookies and writing notes to men who aren't interested in you. You'll have more self-esteem.

Of course, the best thing you can do is try to meet other men, men who do ask you out. Nothing replaces a fantasy relationship better than a *Rules* one! So move on!

Be Smart and Other *Rules* for Dating in School

Remember Janis Ian's song, 'I learned the rules at seventeen, that love was meant for beauty queens?' The fact is, unless you look like Brooke Shields, school can be very rough. There's acne and not fitting into the 'in' crowd, not to mention having to go to discos with a group because you don't have a date. Our *Rules* for school won't guarantee you a date every time, but they will bring out the very best in you and make you more attractive to the opposite sex.

1. If you have really bad acne, go to a dermatologist. Cut out the greasy foods – pizza, crisps, french fries – that make your face oily. Eat fruits and vegetables and drink six to eight glasses of water a day. It also goes without saying that you should never spend Saturday night lying on your bed. Have fun, make plans. Start believing now that you are a creature unlike any other! (See *Rule 1*)
2. Spend your baby-sitting money on manicures and some pretty clothes. Wear makeup, but not too much. The idea is to look pretty, not overdone.

131

3. If you have a crush on a boy, your older brother's friend perhaps, don't act like one of the boys with him. Don't wear a baseball cap and sit around watching a ball game with the group. If he happens to be around, don't talk to him first. Be reserved and slightly mysterious. Let *him* notice you.

4. Always be out, mingling, not indoors, worrying. Go out to the beach, to the movies, to parties, not in your room dwelling on your flaws or quoting Sylvia Plath. When you do go to parties, dances or the beach, don't look wildly around for a boy to talk to you or ask you to dance. Don't chew gum and cackle. Walk erect as if you were balancing a book on your head, look directly in front of you, and seem self-contained even if you're lonely and bored to death.

5. If you have decided to have sex, wait until you are in a steady relationship. Use birth control, specifically a condom. You don't want to end up with an unwanted pregnancy or disease. Impulsive and irresponsible behaviours are not *The Rules*. It can be even cooler and safer to simply wait until you're more mature.

6. Don't smoke, take drugs or drink alcohol, even if a very cool and good-looking boy is pressuring you to do so. Cigarettes are unhealthy, drugs and alcohol are mind altering and addictive and might make you do something that you don't want to do (like sleep with him on the first date). To do *The Rules* you must always be one step ahead. Drugs

and alcohol make you messy and stupid – definitely not *Rules* behaviour.

7. School is a good time to take up sports like jogging, aerobics, swimming or tennis. This is not only good for your body, but also for your social life. Lots of socializing goes on at running tracks and tennis courts. A healthy hobby will give you something to do in the summer. If you have the money, you might think about going to tennis camp where you can meet athletic boys your age. If you spend the summer working, on your days off make sure you go to the beach, get a (safe) tan, wear short shorts and bikinis, and go swimming, play tennis or go rollerblading.

8. *Act* confident even if you don't *feel* it. Notice what kinds of clothes, shoes, bags, jewellery and hairstyles the most popular kids in school are wearing. Don't try to be too different or frugal in this area. You'll feel lousy, so it's not worth it. To see what's hot and what's not, subscribe to a popular magazine for teenagers. Don't let your mind tell you that all of this is superficial and beneath you. (Save your mind for exams and course work.) Don't you like boys who wear Polo shirts and cowboy boots when that's in fashion? Well, they like girls who wear what's on MTV and in the magazines.

6. If the boy you like doesn't ask you out, don't ask him. Better that you go with someone else who asks you or with a group. Start being a *Rules* girl now!

7. If you are lucky enough to have a boyfriend during school, let *him* be the one to worry about the future. Choose a college that's good for you, not necessarily the one he is going to. (Who knows? You could follow him all the way to college only to have him dump you for a prettier girl.) Go to whatever college you like and if he wants to see you, let him travel to *your* campus. Let him call and write to you. Unless you're engaged, date others. Don't spend every weekend with your school boyfriend, as some girls do who have a hard time separating. If you're meant to marry your school sweetheart, it will happen despite the distance between you and despite any other men you meet in college.

Take Care of Yourself and Other *Rules* for Dating in College

If you are going to college soon, we'd like to save you about four years of heartache. Here are seven mistakes not to make, now that *The Rules* are part of your curriculum.

1. Don't look up his timetable and follow him around campus hoping he will eventually notice you. It's great exercise; otherwise, don't bother. Either he noticed *you* or he didn't.

2. Don't hang out in the dining hall for all three dinner shifts hoping to spot him at some point between 4.30 p.m. and 8.00 p.m., and end up gaining the 'freshman 2 stone' instead. (Do you really want to spend your college career in the cafeteria wondering, 'When will so-and-so walk in?')

3. Don't have your girlfriend talk to his best friend and find out how he feels about you or if he even knows who you are, and/or become best friends with the girl on his floor, or do favours for anyone he knows. (Don't waste your time. No one, not even his best friend, can make him like you.)

4. Don't find out what his favourite albums or CDs are and play them all the time and don't wear, say, a Grateful Dead T-shirt if that's his favourite group. (Strange how women think that men are attracted to women who dress like men – sporty and even grungy. Yet, it's always the girls with cute jeans and fashionable shirts that get the guys.) *The Rule* is don't wear clothes to copy men, but to attract them.

5. Don't become a sports fanatic simply because he's on the football or rugby team. The same goes for taking up smoking or drinking because he does those things. Many women we know who sipped Perrier on dates with men who drank alcohol and smoked and are now married to them. When it comes to habits, be yourself.

6. Don't offer to help him with Shakespeare if literature is not his strong suit or type his papers, hoping he'll date you. He either wants to or he doesn't.

7. Don't be stupid about safety! Date rape has become quite rampant in college these days. Be wary. Study in a lounge or library rather than alone with him in his room or off-campus flat. *Always* tell someone your whereabouts so they can keep track of you. *Rules* girls don't take chances. Don't take date rape lightly!

Now that you know what *not* to do, what *should* you do to attract your man on campus?

1. Study! After all, that's what you're there for! Smart is sexy!
2. Eat sensibly, even when your friends are gorging on unlimited cafeteria food and having pizza delivered to their rooms at midnight. We suggest you take fruit from the dining hall to save as a midnight snack. Tell yourself during the pizza party that your jeans will fit tomorrow. Remember, overweight is *not The Rules*.
3. Wear makeup. Read *Vogue* and other popular fashion magazines.
4. Get involved in some extracurricular activity, preferably one that you're interested in and where you can meet men naturally.
5. Don't sit in your room alone on Friday and Saturday nights reading Jean-Paul Sartre. Friday and Saturday nights are for mingling. You can read Sartre on Monday.
6. Pick a subject and a career goal. College is not about picking up your *MRS* degree, although you may very well meet your future husband on campus. Still, you must exercise your brain, both for his sake and yours. Don't be an airhead.

_____

Don't Stand by His Desk and Other *Rules* for the Office Romance

The office is one of the trickiest places to follow *The Rules* because if you are dating someone at work, your professional life and your love life may overlap to some extent. Therefore, you must do *The Rules* strictly so you don't place your job or your relationship (or both) in jeopardy.

Of course, the first rule is to figure out whether or not you are actually *in* an office romance. A lot of men like to flirt with women at the office. They don't think twice about it, it means nothing to them and it should mean nothing to you! (See *Rule 30: Don't Waste Time on Fantasy Relationships*.)

If you have a crush on someone in your office – a co-worker, employee, or your boss – and he's never asked you out, don't try to get his attention. Some dating books have suggested you drink from the water cooler near his office or use the copier closest to his desk or even ask him out to lunch to discuss business. *The Rules* say, do your job and look your best. Don't look for excuses to talk to him or walk by his desk. (You shouldn't have to do any of these things to make him notice you. He either notices you or he doesn't!)

Don't tell yourself that he would have asked you out if you didn't work for the same company. There are enough office romances out there to refute that theory. As we have stated, if it is not a company code, bosses have no problem dating employees and even their own secretaries if they want to. On the other hand, don't count on working for the same company to be the spark that will unite you. Don't stay at the company hoping that one day he will notice you and ask you out. We know women who waited in vain for years for that to happen. *Rules* girls don't hold themselves back for a fantasy relationship.

Now assuming you are dating a co-worker or even your boss, how should you act? Below are fourteen rules for office dating. Do them to the letter because you might have to see this man on a daily basis. There's nothing worse than having to work with a man you dread seeing or who dreads seeing you everyday because you broke rules – or working with him after he drops you! These rules are not just good for the relationship, but for your company and your career. You'll be a better worker if you're not figuring out ways to be with him all day!

1. Do not go to work everyday, motivated by the prospect of seeing him or spending time with him, or you might act out on your feelings. Go to work thinking, how can I work hard today and contribute to my company – or at the very least, how can I not break *The Rules*. Try to be busy, as

opposed to day-dreaming at your desk or, worse, finding reasons to talk to him or see him. (When the urge to stop by his office hits you, begin a new project or stop by a friend's desk to say hello.) If he stops by your desk, be nice, but end the conversation after five or ten minutes unless it's business-related. Just pick up the papers on your desk and say, 'I'd better get back to work!'

2. Work hard, but don't be such a tireless worker that you don't care about your appearance. Don't spend so much time at the office that you have no time for such mundane tasks as taking your clothes to the dry cleaner or getting a manicure. We know women who are smart and attractive, but you can't help but notice the coffee stains on their blazers, their scruffy shoes and untweezed eyebrows. Don't be like that: You're a *Rules* girl!

   Make sure you're wearing fashionable suits and shoes – you want to look as good as you can! Don't wear tights with runs in them – keep extra pairs in your desk drawer in case they rip at work. Shine your shoes. Wear makeup and perfume, but not too much. (It's an office, not a disco!) Remember, you're a creature unlike any other and you care about your looks. Do all of this for yourself but also because you could run into him or someone else at the office.

3. Do not agree to see him on a moment's notice just because you work together. If he stops by your desk and casually asks you to have lunch with him

that day or to have drinks after work that evening, say you'd love to, but can't. Even if you are free for lunch or drinks, don't see him on short notice. He should be asking you out in advance for the weekend.

If you see him on a whim, the relationship will become too casual. He won't think you're special enough to plan in advance to see you. In addition, if you allow the relationship to be on a co-worker level, it could take him years to propose. We know a very attractive woman who accepted last-minute dates from a man she worked with. Several times a week at 6:00 p.m. he would drop by her desk and suggest having drinks. She always said yes. He also couldn't commit to Saturday night dates until Friday or Saturday because *he* 'wasn't sure what he was doing.' She accepted his behaviour because she didn't know there was a better way. It took him six years to propose and their marriage is troubled; he never seems to really make the effort, and she feels taken for granted.

So just because you work at the same company doesn't mean he can see you whenever he feels like it. Don't make it so easy for him. He has to ask you out in advance – otherwise, you're busy! If you work closely together, you should sometimes disappear at lunch hour. Don't tell him where you're going. Remember, he works with you and dates you – that can get a little all-consuming, so you must be doubly careful to remain a little mysterious!

4. Be discreet. Don't talk about the relationship with co-workers. If anyone asks you what you did over the weekend, don't say, 'David and I went hiking.' Just say that you went hiking. Don't answer any questions with 'we'. It may hurt your career to be the subject of office gossip. It's not good for the relationship, either, since no man likes to date a big mouth. Men love privacy. Anything co-workers know about the relationship should come from him!

   Likewise, don't volunteer information to him. For example, don't tell him where you're going on a business trip or who you're having a meeting with unless he specifically asks about either.

5. If you need to talk to the man you are dating about business – perhaps he's your boss – by all means, talk to him! Always be professional and return his calls promptly if it is a business matter. Just check your motives. Is it really necessary to contact him, or are you looking for an excuse to be with him? For example, don't knock on his door to tell him about concert tickets or a lecture on personal growth! If it is work-related, keep the conversation brief and end it first.

   If possible, leave the information with his secretary or in his 'in box'. Write any memos or notes in a businesslike manner. Do not leave love notes or cute Post-it's on his desk. If he needs to talk to you, he can always come to *your* office or leave you a note!

6. He can E-mail you as much as he wants, but don't E-mail him back every time unless it is business-related.

On all non-business E-mails, once for every four of his E-mails is a good rule of thumb. Remember, keep your E-mails brief and breezy and stick to business. This is important, because you never know who has access to your E-mail – it may be read by the head of the company, so keep all romance off the screen and save it for Saturday nights.

7. Don't snoop around his office. You shouldn't even be near his office! Don't ask his secretary who calls him or who he's having lunch with and where. It's none of your business. Besides, she might tell him and he will be annoyed and resent it.

8. Don't make your office a shrine to your relationship. Don't put his photo in a frame on your desk or keep the teddy bear he gave you for Valentine's Day in your office after February 14. It's best to be businesslike.

   Speaking of your office, be neat. Neat is sexy. No one likes to date a slob. So don't be a pack rat. Don't have piles of paper on your desk or stash half-eaten sandwiches in your desk drawer. Don't collect objects or hang memorabilia on the walls. Don't decorate your office like a college dorm room. Don't be cute or juvenile. Be professional.

9. Don't kiss or hold hands at the office. Not only is it unprofessional, it's not good for *The Rules*. He has to ask you out on a date to kiss you or spend quality time with you. Don't agree to go to a hotel with him during your lunch hour. That's not a date and he won't respect you (and you'll come back from

lunch looking rumpled and unbusinesslike). No one wants a reputation – be careful that you don't earn one. Again, he has to ask you out for the weekend for you to take dating him seriously!

10. Don't sleep with your boss or co-worker unless you're in a committed relationship – not just for sex and not to further your career. Bad motives tend to backfire.

    Keep in mind that *The Rules* don't stop because you're out of town. If you're on a business trip together and it would be easy to have sex because you're staying at the same hotel – still say no if you're not in a committed relationship. It may seem tempting – you are away from the office, and who will know? But remember, eventually you have to return home – back to reality – and you'll regret sleeping with him if he isn't serious about you or ignores you when you return to the office.

11. Don't hang out at the office at the end of the day or go to happy hour with the gang after work. You do not want to be thought of as the office party girl, but the kind of girl men marry. And of course don't get drunk at the office Christmas party or at any other party. It's hard to do *The Rules* when you're drunk!

12. If you work in different cities for the same company let him travel to visit you three times before you visit him. If you're sent to his city on business, don't mention getting together. *He* must suggest making plans. If things do get serious, you shouldn't

relocate until you have a commitment/wedding date.

13. Don't stay at the company just because he works there. If you are happy with your job or are interested in other opportunities, pursue them. We don't hold ourselves back for a man. If it's good for your career to leave the company, go! Doing what's good for you will also show him you're independent, not clingy. It might make him miss you and propose faster because he can't see you every day.

14. Do not suggest commuting together even if you live near each other and work at the same company. It must be his suggestion and you should turn him down sometimes just so he doesn't take you for granted and so you can remain mysterious.

Married women have written to us asking how they should behave if they work with their husbands.

We hope they were either already working together when they met, or that it was their husband's idea to work together. Women should never suggest working with their husbands as a way of spending more time with them or checking up on them. It's not *The Rules*, and men hate it. You should only work with your husband if there is a legitimate reason to and/or it was his idea.

Regardless of why you are working together, here are five rules:

1. Do not suggest sharing an office or putting your desks near each other. Any togetherness must come from him.
2. Do not be the one suggesting commuting together.
3. Do not suggest having lunch together. You both need some time apart during the day.
4. Don't spy on him, don't ask his secretary who called, or get upset if he talks to other women.
5. Don't bring up personal business at the office and discourage him if he does. Be professional. Do your job!

Don't Be a Groupie and Other *Rules* for Dating Celebrities or High-Profile Men

It's not everyday that you meet a celebrity or a high-profile man, but it can happen – at a party, on a plane, in the company cafeteria or in a doctor's waiting room. And if you don't know *The Rules* and how to do them, you can easily ruin a once-in-a-lifetime opportunity.

For example, we know a woman who met a famous actor at a fundraiser. He walked right up to her and said, 'You're beautiful. When can we go out?'

Here was the perfect *Rules* beginning – he was obviously attracted to her and made the first move. But not knowing *The Rules*, she gushed, 'Tonight'.

Obviously, that was the wrong answer. When a famous actor says when can I see you, just smile and say, 'Let me think, I don't know …' as if famous actors ask you out all the time. Even if he's ten times busier than you are, act as if you just don't know when you can see him. He must specifically ask you out for a particular night and it cannot be that night or the next night but several nights in advance.

The actor took our friend out to dinner, where she proceeded to tell him how much she admired his work and even asked him to autograph the menu. They spoke for hours (even closed the restaurant) and he hardly had to pressure her to go back to his hotel room. Although she did not have sex with him, she spent the night. He told her he would call her again when he was in town in a few weeks, but she never heard from him. By the time she found out about *The Rules*, it was too late.

What follows are *The Rules* for meeting and dating actors, athletes, famous authors, movie producers, directors, CEOs and other powerful men. Assuming the celebrity or business VIP spoke to you first, here's what to do and what not to do:

1. Take a deep breath. Stay composed.
2. Treat him as you would any other man – a co-worker, your doorman – not the movie star or business tycoon he is.
3. Do not stare at him.
4. Do not light up or act giddy, as if you just won the lottery.
5. Do not carry on like a crazed fan. In other words, do not say anything like, 'Oh my God, I can't believe it's – ! I've seen all your movies!' (Even if you have seen all his movies twice!) Act as if you've been out of the country for the last three years and you're not quite sure who he is, even if he was just on the cover of *People* magazine.
6. Don't ask for his autograph.
7. Don't compliment him, as in 'You look much better in person than on TV.'

8. Don't ask him about his next movie or show any interest in his career (or you'll sound like every other woman he's ever met).

9. If you're an aspiring actress, do not ask for an audition or a part in his movie. If you're looking for work, do not ask this high-powered executive for a job in his company. Do not ask for his business card or offer to send him your CV or movie script.

10. Do not ask him to do you a favour, such as donate money to your favourite charity or give you tickets to his show or a free copy of his book.

11. Act interested but not spellbound. Movie stars and CEOs are typically hounded and drooled over. So leave him alone. After five minutes or ten minutes of conversation about whatever he wants to talk about, say, 'Oh, look at the time, I must leave now. It was nice meeting you' and walk away. Do not spend the evening talking to this man. Do not agree to go out with him that night, even if he's leaving the country the next morning. (He can always call you – they have phones in other countries, too.)

12. Do not seem impressed by his Armani suit, limo or entourage.

13. If you meet a performer and he offers you a ticket to see his concert or show as a first date, politely decline. Attending his show is not a date. If he wants to see you the night of the show, he must pick you up afterward and take you out.

14. If you're dating a sports star, don't run around the country wearing his jersey and attending all his

> games until you're in a committed relationship. Even then, he still must ask you out on dates to spend time with you.

15. Once you're actually dating a CEO or celebrity, don't see him whenever and wherever it's convenient for him because *he* has a busy schedule. He still has to ask you out in advance and you must turn him down politely if he expects to see you only on his terms – otherwise he will take you for granted. Celebrities are used to being spoiled, but you're a *Rules* girl.

16. Of course, it's tempting to drop your friends and family and revolve your whole life around this famous man. By following *The Rules*, you must still live your own life, see him only two to three times a week – until he proposes.

17. If he's handsome or widely popular, expect that other women might write to him, call him and throw themselves at him in public. Do not get angry or show jealousy or insecurity when this happens. Do not be possessive in public. If he pursued you and you're doing *The Rules*, their advances won't matter. He'll still want you.

18. Be discreet. Do not call the tabloids and tell them you're dating a celebrity, as a way of announcing to other women that he's your man – that doesn't work anyway – and don't talk to reporters if they call you. That would be self-serving, possibly hurtful or embarrassing to him, and might ruin any chances of his continuing to see you.

19. Don't try to become too friendly with his secretary, publicist or limo driver in an effort to keep tabs on him or so they put in a good word for you.
20. Don't seem overly interested in his fame, his wealth or the limelight. *Rules* girls are not groupies.

Keep in mind, sometimes a star is *not* your Mr Right, and sometimes your Mr Right is not a star. If you truly want things to work out between you, take things slowly, get to know him and determine whether you love *him* or his image.

Rules for Turning a Friend Into a Boyfriend

You've been friends for ages. Now, for whatever reason, you've decided he's 'The One'. Can you turn a friend into a boyfriend?

Only if *he* really always liked you, but you or circumstances prevented the friendship from developing further. For example, *you* never wanted anything more until recently, or you were both dating other people. Maybe you couldn't imagine him as a boyfriend because of age differences (he's much older or younger than you), personality differences (he's artsy, you're a business-type), or you come from different backgrounds.

How can you be sure he always liked you as more than a friend if you've just been friends?

There are certain things a friend does or says when he is drawn to you. For example:

He always just happens to be in your neighbourhood or business area. He likes to watch his favourite programmes in your flat. He likes your TV set better. If you are co-workers, he's frequently drinking water from the fountain near your desk. If you're in college, he's always hanging outside of your dorm room or is often at the dining hall when you're there.

The bottom line: when a man is attracted to you, he finds ways – excuses – to be near you. We're not exaggerating when we say, whoever's near you likes you! You don't have to look far or wide to find him. He's always hanging around. You can't get rid of him!

When a friend wants to date you, he doesn't talk about other women, even if he's dating someone else. He never seems to notice other women, even your very attractive friend. If, in fact, he is attracted to other women, he tells everyone but you. Around you, the words will just not come out, they stick in his throat.

While he's private about his own love life, he wants to know about yours and asks a lot of questions. He wants to know the type of guy you like to date and what you like to do on Saturday nights. He makes it sound as if he's just curious, *no big deal*, *of course*, but he's really figuring out how he's going to use that information to make a move one day. He thinks anyone you're dating is not good enough for you. He'll even put them down ('His father got him the job').

When a male friend is really interested in you, he tries to be helpful. He offers to show you how to play tennis or how to work the computer. He might help you move your stuff from one flat to another or listen to your work or roommate problems without expecting anything in return. In fact, he never expects you to help him with anything, unless it's an excuse to stay connected to you.

If he likes you as more than a friend, he'll tease you,

flirt with you and make you laugh. He thinks your shortcomings are cute.

He means more than he says. He tries to be cool around you, but he's really quite nervous.

When a male friend is *not* interested in you romantically, he behaves quite differently. He's calm, rational, matter-of-fact. You can take everything he does and says at face value.

He asks you for advice about dating another woman because he *really* wants your advice! He's simply interested in a woman's perspective. He's not secretly in love with you or bringing it up to get closer to you. He talks freely about liking other women. He might even say in front of you, 'She's really cute.' He doesn't think he could be hurting your feelings because you're his friend. You're like his sister – there's no sexual undercurrent.

When a male friend likes you as a friend, he's not that interested in your love life. He's satisfied with your friendship. If you're not dating anyone, he might offer to fix you up with someone, but he doesn't want to go out with you himself. He doesn't want to start anything, he feels no spark.

If you're having a problem with the guy you're dating, he will try to help you 'work it out', as opposed to helping you get out of the relationship! He's not angry if he sees you with other men because he's not interested in you romantically. He *wants* to see you happy. If he's a little jealous when you have a boyfriend, it's in the same way a close girlfriend might be. Your relationship reminds him of what he doesn't have and takes time away from your friendship with him. It's friendship loss, not a romantic loss. This, however, doesn't mean he wants you. You'd know if he did – if you thought about it honestly.

When a male friend is just a friend, he helps you as much as you help him. He'll show you how to read a financial statement, you'll teach him how to cook. Everything's Dutch treat. It's a mutually beneficial relationship.

A male friend might even be your best friend – someone who would be there in a pinch if you ever needed him. He would lend you money to pay your rent, visit you in the hospital if you had an accident, or come to the funeral if a family member died. *But he doesn't look down the street when you walk away, try to stare at you when you're not looking, or secretly dream about having sex with you. And such feelings on a man's part are essential in the beginning of a romantic relationship!*

If he likes you only as a friend, there is nothing you can do about becoming his girlfriend. Don't try to convince him by having a heart-to-heart talk about your feelings because it will probably put a strain on your friendship. He will feel awkward or sorry for you, but he still won't feel a spark. He may try a 'let's sleep together' once or twice. But it won't mean much to him and you, if not both of you, will come to regret it.

Worse yet, the two of you may decide to date or even get married at your initiation. But because he never felt a spark, your marriage will be more of a friendship and if you want more than that you will constantly be unhappy. You will be doubting your looks and your sexuality and complain, 'He never notices me.' Your self-confidence really plummets when you sleep with or get involved with a man who only really wanted a friendship. It's a bad road to travel. Don't even try it.

Just do *The Rules* – not to get him to like you since you can't – but for your self-esteem. Do *The Rules* so that your whole life isn't about this unavailable friend. Don't call him. When he calls, get off the phone in ten minutes. Don't play therapist when he talks about his girlfriend problems. More important, try to meet other men. You're better off forcing yourself to go to social events to meet your possible husband than forcing yourself on this friend.

But if you think he may be interested in you, you can casually mention that you're having boyfriend problems, not seeing your boyfriend anymore or that you're not dating anyone in particular. See how he reacts. If he's interested, he'll ask you out, and then start doing *The Rules*.

Don't talk to him like a friend – like Elaine on *Seinfeld* – but be light, feminine and mysterious. Don't tell him all your problems. Don't start pursuing him with calls, notes and dinner invitations. Don't think you can say or do anything you want – call him whenever you feel like it or suddenly try to increase the time you spend together – because you were platonic friends. Concentrate on making your relationship a *Rules* relationship. Keep in mind, the dynamics will be a little different now. For example, if he's from out-of-town and used to crashing on your couch when he visits you, now you should be the first to say, 'It's been great, but I have a really big day tomorrow,' and end the evenings first.

Now that you want him, you may be tempted to go to the other extreme – call him all the time, talk about your change of heart, refer to him as your soul mate, talk about marriage or the future – and drive him away. Men don't like to be overwhelmed, *even by women they like*.

Many women who wake up one day and decide that their male friend is their soul mate have been known to come on too strong and overwhelm their friend. Remember, part of the reason he liked you is that you didn't really notice him and never pursued him! You've been a challenge – not because you were trying to do *The Rules* – but because you were truly not interested. You were naturally indifferent.

Therefore, when you start to date, you must not let the fact that he always liked you stop you from doing certain rules. For example, don't see him at the last minute or all the time. Don't start knitting him sweaters or talk about marriage or moving in. Okay, you've decided he's 'The One'. But until he's decided you're 'The One' and courts you and proposes, you have to do *The Rules* – or you might ruin a good thing!

Second Chances – *Rules* For Getting Back an Ex

If you are someone who read *The Rules* and thought, 'If only I had done *The Rules* on my old boyfriend' or 'So that's why he wouldn't commit!' then this *Rule* is for you.

You may not have seen him in months or even years, but now you're convinced he could have been 'The One'. You didn't know any better and you blew it … and now you could kick yourself! If only you had known *The Rules* back then!

You want him back. At the very least, you want to give the relationship a second chance. You want to do *The Rules* this time and see what happens. You're wondering if there's any hope. You want to know what to do next, if anything.

Before you make a move, take a deep breath, calm down and forgive yourself. Realize that what you're going through is very common – regretting the past, wishing you had behaved differently with a certain man, thinking he's the one that got away and you'll never meet anyone better. We've received hundreds of letters from women that begin with: 'I wish I had had this book ten years ago when I was dating (fill in the blank).' These women either just didn't know they should behave a certain way with men, or they instinctively knew they should but didn't have the strength to do it without specific guidelines and support.

Of course all you care about now that you've read *The Rules* is, can you get him back?

It depends.

If you initiated the relationship – spoke to him first, asked him out – and he eventually ended it, then it's not only over, it was never meant to be. Don't call him or write to him or try to contact him in any way to say you've changed and want a second chance. He didn't really want you in the first place. Forget him and move on!

But if he pursued you and you broke rules – for example, you were possessive, saw him every night, or moved in with him and he broke it off because he felt suffocated – there may be hope. There's one way to find out and we call it 'One Call for Closure'.

Call him *once* when you're sure he's not home, so you get his answering machine. Calling when he's not in is crucial; you don't want to make him uncomfortable if he doesn't want to hear from you or is involved with someone else or even married. Leaving a message also allows him to call you if and when *he* wants to, which is the best start for any conversation between you. Your message gives him time to think and the option of not calling, which you must give him. Of course, if his answering machine says, 'We're not home right now' and you hear a woman's voice chiming in, do not leave a message. Leave him alone and go on with your life.

Assuming he's not involved with someone, we suggest you leave the following message: 'Hi, it's (your name). I just wanted to say hello, to see how you're doing. You can reach me at (phone number).' That's it!

If you don't hear from him, it's over. Don't call again to make sure he got the message. He got the message. His answering machine isn't broken. Don't write to him or track him down at work, home, his favourite bar or the gym. That's called stalking. Forget all about him and move on. You must work on accepting the way he feels and not dwelling on the past and what might have been. Don't berate yourself; if you were supposed to end up with him, you would have. Tell yourself there's someone else out there for you, try to date others and keep doing *The Rules*.

If he does call, don't automatically assume he's rekindling the romance. He might just be returning your call, being polite, nothing deep. So try not to get too excited or show how happy you are to hear from him. Be cool, cordial. Say, 'Oh hi. How are you?' Don't say, 'I was hoping you'd call.'

If he asks why you called, just say, 'Oh, I wondered how you were doing and wanted to say hello.' Keep the conversation light ... business, holidays and so on. Don't ask him if he ever thinks about you or misses you, if he's seeing anyone new. After ten minutes, say, 'Well, I have to get going. It was nice talking to you.' Don't stay on the phone for thirty minutes or an hour, waiting and hoping he will suggest drinks. If he doesn't ask you out within ten minutes, he's not interested. Remember, if he *is* interested but needs more than ten minutes to ask out an ex-girlfriend, he can always call you again!

If he does ask you out, say yes if it's for a future date – it need not be a Saturday night the first time you meet, but it should be at least three days in advance. You want to let him know that your life didn't stop since the two of you split and that your calendar is full.

Look very, very good when you meet him. Extra care with your makeup, pretty outfit. Don't dress down as if it's your 200th date, even if technically, it is. Be light, casual, upbeat. Needless to say, don't have a heavy discussion about your relationship or the past, unless he brings up the subject. Even if he talks about the way it was, try not to dwell on it. Discuss general topics such as what you have both been doing professionally, if he still runs three miles every morning, and so on. Keep the date on a 'let's catch up' level, as opposed to a 'what you've been through since the break-up' level. By the way, you should not tell him how much or how little you've dated since the break-up. Be honest, but mysterious.

Don't get terribly serious. Don't tell him that you now realize all the mistakes you've made since the relationship with him ended and how much you've changed and how you want another chance. It's too intense. Besides, it's easy to tell someone how much you've changed. The important part is actually *being* a changed person when he dates you!

Don't tell him that you've read *The Rules* and now realize what you did wrong – that you were too needy, that you shouldn't have got mad when he went out with the guys, and that you'll never be that way again. Simply be light. Try to be the girl he originally fell in love with.

End the date first.

Don't go back to his house or invite him to yours or even think of having sex with him that night. *Remember, this is a first date. If anything, you must be extra strict with this man. He dumped you once, he can hurt you again.*

If this is to be a *Rules* relationship, he must call you and ask you out for Saturday night from now on. Seeing you either awakened a desire to date you again and to renew the relationship, or it didn't. The only way to find out is if he calls you and asks you out. You should not ask him if he missed you or if he wants to get back together. If he is to pursue you, he should not know exactly how you feel about him. He should think, 'She called me one day. She might be interested, but I'm not sure. Maybe she was just bored or found an old photo of us.' Remain mysterious – if he thinks that you've decided he's 'The One', he could get scared.

If he calls, you must do *Rule 10: How to Act on Dates 1, 2, and 3* and *Rule 11: How to Act on Dates 4 through Commitment Time*. Treat him like a new boyfriend – don't talk about the past or act too chummy. For example, you should not call his family, even if you met his parents and sister twenty times when you were dating. Remember, you've been apart. He has to invite you to any social events with his family and friends all over again.

If you meet him for dinner and he never calls again, he may not have felt a strong enough spark. Maybe he thought about it, but never got around to picking up the phone. Men can be that way. Maybe he's involved with someone else, but didn't tell you and met you for old time's sake.

We know of several women who contacted old boyfriends for various reasons – to make amends for the past, to discuss a business problem, or to try to start over. In each case, these men met them for drinks, said they had a great time and hoped they could stay good friends, and then never called again.

We can only say that if this happens to you, you must try to accept that it's over for him and move on.

Now what if this man happens to be your ex-husband and you've decided you want him back?

Again, it depends. If *he* initiated the divorce, you can make 'One Call for Closure' and then follow the plan (outlined earlier) for getting back an ex-boyfriend. But don't start making room in your wardrobe. When a man initiates a divorce, he's usually gone! It's over and out.

However, if you initiated the divorce but are now sorry and miss him, there is hope, especially if you are still in contact with your ex and sense that he would be open to a reconciliation – maybe you have kids together and he lingers a while when he comes by on weekends to pick them up or just seems to find reasons to call you, to be friends, to be in your life. But you're wondering, how do you go about telling him you want him back without making a fool of yourself or risking rejection?

We suggest you simply weave the following question into a friendly conversation the next time you see him or he calls: 'Have you ever had second thoughts about our divorce?' *That's it. Don't say another word.* Don't get sentimental and weepy and pour your heart out. He must take it from there, give you some indication that he would also like a reconciliation, whether it be then or at some point in the future when he's had a chance to sort it out. Whatever you do, don't rush him. Let him proceed at his own pace. He may suggest having dinner or drinks to talk things over, but these must be his overtures. You've done your part. Now it's up to *him*.

We've outlined our suggestions for getting back an ex. But don't be too upset if your old boyfriend or ex-husband just won't come back. Remember, there was a reason the relationship didn't work out before, so don't romanticize it. Also, comfort yourself with the knowledge that it's usually easier to do *The Rules* on a new man than an ex.

Sometimes trying to rekindle an old flame works, but frequently the best advice we can give a woman who thinks she's still in love with her ex is *Next*!

Don't Date a Married Man

Dating married (or unavailable) men is not only an obvious waste of time, but also it's dishonest and stupid. So why do so many women do it? Some feel it's better than dating no one, some find the very wrongness and danger of it (the secret hotel rendezvous) fun and exciting and some hang on to the hope that one day the men will leave their wives for them.

All these women suffer from low self-esteem or why would they settle for so little? We are not big advocates of therapy, but we believe it would be worth fifty pounds per hour to find out why you would do this to yourself.

When you date a married man, you basically spend your life waiting for him to get separated. The deadline keeps changing from September to Christmas, then Easter, then May Day. You wait and you sit by the phone on the off chance that his wife took the kids to her parents' house and he can spend an hour or two with you. And you cry when he can't see you on Valentine's Day or on his wedding anniversary or his wife's birthday. You are always second. In the beginning, affairs are full of promise and great sex. By the end, you are always crying on the shoulders of girl-friends and wishing his wife would die.

You will not get much sympathy from us. Dating married men is dishonest and totally contrary to *The Rules*. We do not take what is not ours. We don't date married men because then we get a reputation for it and no one will trust us around their boyfriends or husbands.

If you have recently met a married man that you are mad about, then you must practise self-restraint. If he is everything you ever wanted in a husband, be friends with him and hope he gets divorced. Until then, you must say to yourself that a single man like him exists somewhere out there for you. Then you must get busy, go to a singles dance, answer a personal ad or put one in a magazine, ask your friends to fix you up with someone. Take action. Join a gym, a church or syna-gogue, or do volunteer work at a hospital. Never sit around dreaming about him or you might end up acting on your thoughts.

Dating a married man is easy because you can fanta-size about his future availability. But, at the risk of sounding preachy, it bears repeating that you won't be at peace if you date a married man. Even if he leaves his wife, how do you know he'll actually marry you?

You're a *Rules* girl! Your life is never on the edge because of a man. Either a man is available and in love with you or he's taken and you have nothing to do with him romantically. You are not desperately waiting in the wings for his situation to change. You are not someone who waits and hopes while he takes his wife and kids to Disney World. You have a life of your own.

Lest you think we are being naive, we know that extramarital affairs happen all the time and that married men do at times divorce their wives and marry the girl they've been seeing on the side. We know one such woman who waited five years for a man to break up with his wife. They are now very happily married. She was very lucky. Are you willing to take that chance?

Don't Be a Rebound Girl and Other *Rules* for Dating a Man Who is Separated

As we explained in *Rule 37*, *Rules* girls don't date married men. It's not honest, he's not yours and you could waste a lot of time waiting for him to leave his wife, if he ever does.

Many women, however, have called us to say they are dating a married man. To these women, all we can suggest is that they find the courage – pray for it, do whatever it takes – to stop seeing him. Dating a married man is like driving down a dead-end street – it gets you nowhere. Better to date him when he's divorced and available. So don't call him, don't write him letters, don't initiate encounters and don't meet him at a moment's notice.

Be sure the man you are dating is at the very least separated from his wife. But don't assume he is. How can you tell? If he doesn't give you his home number, tells you the best way to get in touch with him is by his beeper or gives you a phone number but he's never there when you call, doesn't introduce you to family or friends, and acts on the secretive side, then you must wonder! Something is off. Be on the alert. He might be trying to juggle two lives. You'll find out soon enough if you do *The Rules* and pay attention.

So now, hopefully, you are dating a man who is *really* separated. That can be messy enough! There's his ex-wife, money issues, lawyers and sometimes complicated custody battles. It might feel like walking into the middle of a movie. Are you willing to deal with all these issues and a possibly lengthy courtship?

If you are, here are some rules:

In addition to following all the rules for dating a single man, you must *pay attention* to what he says about why his marriage didn't work out and how it might affect his chances of marrying and *staying* married to you. If he doesn't talk about the break-up, try to find out (without being too obvious) whether it was his idea or hers to get a divorce.

This information is important. If the divorce was his idea, it probably means he isn't hung up on his ex — a good sign. On the other hand, it also shows that he is capable of leaving a woman and that he could walk out on you one day. If you have been able to surmise that it wasn't a *Rules* marriage — in other words, she pursued him — and your relationship is, you have nothing to worry about. He just wanted out of a bad marriage.

But if you think he just picked up and left one day for no good reason, keep your eye on him. He could be bad news. Fortunately, *The Rules* will help you screen out any disturbing behaviour and inconsistencies — skipping a Saturday night date here and there, a few no-shows, forgetting your birthday — long before you walk down the aisle.

If it was his wife's idea to end the marriage, realize that he may still have feelings for her and there's a chance they could get back together. This is particularly true if he is newly separated – say, under six months. He may be dating you merely as a *distraction* – as a way of helping himself get over his ex. If he talks about her all the time when he's with you, then he's not crazily in love with you. Remember, you want to be his *Rules* girl, not his rebound girl!

So be on the lookout for signs that he finds excuses to contact her, still fights with her a lot and gets very emotional about the separation. That's not how he should behave when he's over her and in love with you! When a man is not interested in staying with an ex, he has little to do with her and does not try to prolong the divorce for any reason. He just wants it over.

Whatever the case is, don't play therapist to his marital problems. If he always wants to talk about the break-up, listen politely for a little while here and there, but don't give him advice and don't help him put down his ex-wife if he has a habit of doing so. He can put down his ex-wife, but you shouldn't. Don't show jealousy or seem too interested if he is in contact with her. The less you appear to care, the better.

Don't resolve to be the 'nicer second wife' if and when he marries you. For example, if he complains that his ex-wife was too busy with her career and not there enough for him, you might think you shouldn't do *The Rules*, that you can't end dates first because he's so needy and you should put him before your career. You might decide to see him constantly, cook meals on the weekends for him to have during the week — literally, *take care of him*. This is a big mistake. We know women who played therapist/nurse, became the *woman who understands*, spent years on a man, only to see him remarry someone just like his ex! Whatever he may say about his ex-wife, remember, he married her. On some level, he likes that type. You can't always go by what a man says — it's what he does that counts. Just do *The Rules* and be true to yourself.

Remember, when you are dating a man who is separated, it is easy to get caught up in his problems, his schedule, his timetable, his needs. For example, he might say that he doesn't want to remarry 'for a while' until things settle down or that he wants to wait until his children can handle all the changes, not to mention a stepmum.

Be understanding, but not *too* understanding. *Rules* girls don't wait forever. If he is serious about marrying you, there is no reason why he shouldn't be divorced within a year after meeting you or as soon as possible. You should be engaged within six months after his divorce comes through. You should have a wedding date set soon after you are engaged.

Keep in mind that these are general guidelines — don't be difficult or inflexible if there are children involved or extenuating circumstances. You should only be concerned if he avoids the whole subject of marriage or wants you to live with him first. In either case, you might have to re-evaluate or stop seeing him for a while. *Rules* girls don't wait indefinitely for men to sort out their lives. Don't spoil him by waiting. If he needs more than two years to remarry, he may not be *your* Mr Right.

The fact that he has children should not change this time structure too much, but it does mean that you need to be especially considerate of his relationship with his kids. Sometimes you really must take a backseat, sometimes you have to exhibit the patience of a saint.

Don't ask to meet his children. He must include you in that part of his life when he's ready and wants to. You never want to be in a situation where his kids resent you or blame you for his marital problems or feel that you are taking their father away from them. He should deal with their anger. He should explain to them that he loves you and that his marriage failed on its own, that it had nothing to do with you. You shouldn't get involved.

Don't get jealous if at times he puts his children before you – i.e., he can't have Sunday brunch with you because he must see his son play soccer. His desire to be a good father, his loyalty to his children are qualities to be proud of and admire – not to be resentful of. Bite your tongue, stay busy. Don't make him feel that he has to choose between you and his children. If you plan to be their stepmum one day, then you must also think of their needs, in addition to your own.

Although we are asking you to be considerate about his relationship with his kids – and divorce can be traumatic for any child – we are not telling you to be a doormat. We know men who ask their girlfriends to be baby-sitters or take their daughter ice-skating, but they never propose. You are not a baby-sitter or the girlfriend who is there for him, who waits and waits forever.

Dating a man who is separated can be difficult. But by doing *The Rules*, you don't put your life on hold indefinitely. You don't make excuses to yourself about why he won't remarry or why he needs years to heal from his divorce. When you do *The Rules*, a man who is separated recovers pretty quickly and happily marries you!

Slowly Involve Him in Your Family and Other *Rules* for Women with Children

If you are a divorced or single woman with children, you should follow all *The Rules*. In addition, be especially careful when dating not to go on about all the pain from your first marriage or talk too much about your children.

When you meet a man at a dance or social situation, it isn't really necessary to mention your children at all. Let him take your phone number, then wait until he calls for you to gently weave it into the conversation. Don't say in a serious tone, 'I need to tell you something.' Remember in *Rule 24: Don't Open Up Too Fast*, we advise you to tell him about yourself very informally. Just casually say, 'Oh, that's my son playing the piano' or something like that.

If and when he does ask you out for Saturday night, don't say, 'Nine on Saturday is great, but I'll have to call the baby-sitter.' Don't fill him in on the details of bringing up children or how your ex-husband was supposed to baby-sit and is just so unreliable! It isn't necessary for a man to know you haven't had your alimony payments for the last three months and Tommy really needs new trainers. Simply say, 'Saturday at nine is great.' At this point he is interested in *you*, not your family or your problems.

Please do not take this advice the wrong way. We are not telling you to be ashamed of your past or your children. Just wait a while before involving him. On your first few dates, it would be wise to meet your date in a restaurant so you don't have to introduce him to your children. This is as much for your date's sake as your child's. Your child should not have to meet every Tom, Dick and Harry you date, only the serious contenders. Let the man be the one to bring up meeting your children. Make him curious about seeing them. Meeting your children should be an honour, not a routine occurrence. Just like the way you hold back on other things in the beginning of your relationship, this too should take time. Make him work (again? yes) for the privilege of meeting your loved ones.

On the other hand, don't use motherhood as an excuse not to get out there and mingle. Having children often means being in situations with married people and you might feel like a fifth wheel among all the couples you meet at PTA meetings. But remember that there are plenty of single fathers out there who want to remarry. So go to PTA meetings with a smile on your face and wearing a nice outfit. Socialize wherever you go with your child. You never know.

Starting Over –
Rules for the Mature Woman

If you are an older woman, *The Rules* may come as no surprise to you. You probably agree with our ideas more than your twenty-five or thirty-five year old daughters. After all, when you were dating thirty or forty years ago – before the full advent of feminism, Dutch treat and the sexual revolution – *The Rules* was the accepted way to date. It was the only way. Back then, you didn't call men, ask them out, sleep with them on the first date or live together before marriage. You didn't think twice about it either, it just wasn't done!

But that doesn't mean you did *The Rules* in their entirety, and it doesn't mean you don't have things to learn, especially if your first marriage was a disaster.

Your mother may have told you not to chase men, but did she tell you to pursue a career and/or interests, to develop boundaries and self-esteem, and not to make a man the centre of your life or accept his bad behaviour? Did she tell you to marry for love (not just to get out of the house or to be taken care of financially)? If she didn't, you need *The Rules*.

We have heard from older women who said that their first marriages ended in divorce – not necessarily because they pursued their husbands, but for other reasons that simply would not have occurred if they had done *The Rules*.

For example, they married a good friend – someone whom they felt affection for, but not passion – and their marriage and sex life reflected it. They married for financial security and were miserable emotionally. They married because of social pressures to do so – they didn't want to be spinsters. They did not recognize the signs, or they chose to ignore them. They thought, 'My love will change him,' and married an alcoholic, a gambler or a womaniser and lived to regret it. Love was not enough. They didn't create an interesting life of their own and became completely dependent on their husbands, which drove them away.

These women did not necessarily chase these men, but they did not do *The Rules* either. *The Rules* are not just about getting married, but about marrying Mr Right and having a fulfilling life of your own.

So if you find yourself in the dating market again because you are divorced or a widow, use what your mother taught you – don't chase men – but also do *The Rules* – create a life of your own and only date and marry men you truly care for who treat you well. Don't marry believing you will change him. If he is a little abusive or puts you down in any way before marriage – it will only get worse.

If you are from the old school, not calling a man or sleeping with him on the first date is probably easy for you. So you must work on other changes that could prevent you from catching Mr Right.

For example, have you stopped caring about your appearance – gained weight, stopped wearing makeup, cut down on salon visits?

If you're divorced, are you bitter about men because of your failed marriage? Or too eager and available (not challenging and mysterious) when men do show interest?

If you're a widow, do you feel hopeless about finding a love as great as your first husband? Have you stopped socializing? Or when you do go out occasionally, are you unenthusiastic?

If some or all of the above is the case, here are some rules for you to work on:

Don't let yourself go: Remember, you are a creature unlike any other. This rule applies to older women as much as twenty-five year olds. It has nothing to do with age. It's mental. Think you're beautiful and worthwhile ... and you will be! Think positive. Keep your mind occupied with interesting ideas, activities, people and reading material and you will be interesting. You'll have something to talk about on dates other than you doctors' visits and grandchildren.

Whatever you do, don't neglect your appearance. There is no reason you shouldn't do everything you can to look attractive. Don't console yourself with excess food or alcohol or painkillers. Eat right, exercise daily and wear pretty clothes. Read books by Helen Gurley Brown (*The Late Show*) and Joan Rivers (*Bouncing Back*) that focus on being positive and exercising to fight off ageing. Try to emulate them or anyone else you know who is your age and in good shape. Be old-fashioned about dating, but youthful about your attitude and looks.

Socialize: You must. If you are recently divorced or widowed, your feelings probably range from lonely and lost to bitter and confused, especially if your husband died or left you for a younger woman. You might be suffering from grief, fear and panic. Perhaps you haven't dated in thirty years and don't know where to begin. Of course, you must allow yourself time to grieve – grieving is natural and healthy – but don't let it go on too long.

If you want to remarry or at least have a loving companion, you must make every effort to meet men. Instead of believing that your life is over and all you have to look forward to is grandchildren, tell yourself that there are plenty of divorced men and widowers out there, and go where you can meet them.

We understand that this is not always easy or pleasant. You would much rather stay at home and watch TV, call your children, knit, cook or read a book, but don't become a recluse, or spend every free evening going to the movies and dinner with other women. Don't bury yourself in canasta, card games or mah-jong with your single friends. These are all pleasant ways to pass time and you should do them sometimes, but they are no way to meet men!

Motivate yourself to take social actions by thinking of spending your old age with a loving man, not only as a companion to your married couple friends and your children. Think of how a romance will brighten up your life, and the benefits of spending nights, weekends and holidays with a man.

Where to meet men? Try everything. Go to museums, church/synagogue, holidays/cruises for your age group, or get involved in a charity or a sport such as golf where men are sure to be found. You must force yourself!

Be on the lookout for men who are newly single. Keep in mind that men who have been married for most of their adult lives are often lost and searching for someone to fill that void. Show up wherever they may be found but remember, they must approach you!

If you can't find a woman to go to social events with, go alone. In fact, you might be better off alone! Older men who are themselves not so confident socially may feel uncomfortable invading a group of women. So if you do attend a party or lecture with a group, at least stand a little apart from the other women you came with so you look approachable. Take care to appear relaxed no matter how you really feel. For example, don't clutch your handbag tightly against your chest as if you are trying to ward off a mugger.

Be happy and carefree on dates: You probably have had your share of life's difficulties and maybe even some physical ailments. Possibly you're worried because your daughter is getting divorced, your back bothers you, your husband died and left you with big bills, you have high blood pressure or had a brush with cancer. You may have plenty to complain about, but try to complain to your women friends, not to a man you are dating. Be cheerful and light. Don't let him think that you are desperate to remarry, concerned about money or feel lost without a man. It's not good to seem desperate.

Once you start dating someone you like, almost all *The Rules* apply:

Don't call him – of course, you already knew that! – but you can return his calls. While older men enjoy the chase, it's a different kind of hunt. It's no longer a bungee jump! They're not looking for that kind of a thrill. They're not trying to have children with you. They're older, they're tired, they've been through many things, so you can call them back ... the next day. (Try to use the twenty-four-hour rule; wait twenty-four hours before returning the call.)

Don't accept a last-minute date and don't see him unless it's for the weekend. If he's always asking you out for tea on Tuesday, he doesn't think you're that special or he has a girlfriend. Let him pick you up and take you to dinner.

Don't mention your children or grandchildren and show pictures of them or ask him to meet them unless he suggests it, and don't ask about his children or ex-wife unless he brings them up. Don't volunteer information about your ex-husband. If he asks about your divorce, just say the relationship didn't work out. If you are a widow, don't get too emotional or show how much you are suffering. This will be hard, but you must!

Keep it casual in the beginning and end the date first. Wait until you are in a committed relationship – he is calling you regularly and asking you out for Saturday nights for several months – to become very involved or go away with him.

Don't buy him expensive gifts or pamper him, even if you are a wealthy woman and can afford to do so. Also, if you have more money than he does and he wants to marry you, don't be shy about asking him to sign a prenuptial agreement. (Of course, if he asks you to sign a prenup, go ahead. You are not marrying for money.)

Older women might not necessarily want to remarry. The reasons are usually children and money. But if you do want to get married and he doesn't, then you must pull back a little – stop seeing him for a few weeks, go on a separate holiday, give him an ultimatum, whatever shakes him up a little – and see how he responds.

If getting remarried is not that important to you – if it's love and companionship you want, not a wedding and lifestyle you crave – then it's fine to live with him or go steady forever! You can act married – go away on holidays together and split the expenses. You can even spend a whole winter with him in your condo in Florida.

So long as he is calling you, making you feel special – weekend dinners and flowers on holidays – and is civil

to your children, you don't have to walk down the aisle
again. For you, the second time around is about having
someone you love who loves you to spend your golden
years with.

Practise, Practise, Practise!
(or, Getting Good at *The Rules*)

How does one get good at *The Rules*? Unfortunately, the same way one gets good at playing the piano or tennis or anything else. Practice, practice and more practice!

Once you're truly convinced you need *The Rules*, you should read this book over and over again until you've practically memorized it, then practise the principles as much as possible. Don't expect to get them right the first time or every time. We didn't. We broke rules, got hurt and then eventually got serious and did *The Rules* as they are written.

Don't be discouraged. Just keep practising! Try *The Rules* on all men at all times. Don't even say hello first to your doorman or the butcher at the deli. Let them say hello to you first and then just smile. Don't ignore them or anyone else, just practise responding rather than starting any conversation. Then later, when a man says to you, 'I bet you were a real heartbreaker at school,' you will instinctively smile and say nothing. If, however, you are so used to blabbering all the time, then you might start explaining that you were thirty pounds heavier in school, never had a boyfriend and hardly ever went out. If he is planning to marry you,

you will eventually tell him all about your unpopular days and by that time it won't really matter. We find that most women regret spilling their innermost feelings and thoughts on the first few dates. There will be less to regret if you learn to be quiet and mysterious more often. Reread *Rules 24* and *25*.

When the urge to call him comes, call a friend, your mother, the weather channel, walk the dog, write a letter, answer a personal ad, anything, until the urge passes, and it will. Call a friend who recently broke *The Rules* to remember how painful it is to chase a man. If you must call a man, better that you call a friendly ex-boyfriend than the current man of your dreams. The old relationship is over and there's not much to lose, but your new flame may lose interest in you if you pursue him.

The good news, girls, is that the more you practise *The Rules*, the easier it gets. If it's painful, remember, none of us do them perfectly. But try to do the best you can. Ending a phone conversation after ten minutes seemed cruel and impossible for us in the beginning, but the more we used a timer and did it anyway, the more natural it became to say, 'It's been nice talking to you, but I really have to run.'

It's not necessary to have a high IQ to do *The Rules*, just a certain degree of determination. In fact, highly educated girls have the hardest time with *The Rules*. They tend to think all this is beneath them. They'll say, 'I went to university. I'm not playing these games' or 'I'm in management. I believe in being up front with men about my needs, my opinions and who I really am. I refuse to be demure and smile when I don't *feel* like it.'

If you think you're too smart for *The Rules*, ask yourself, 'Am I married?' If not, why not? Could it be that what you're doing isn't working? Think about it.

But even if you're not desperate to get married right away, you never know when you'll change your mind. We've all met women who are certain in their twenties that they don't want two kids and a house in the suburbs. They tell us that their career, friends and assorted romantic relationships are fine with them. So they don't bother to play hard to get when they meet men. They treat men like women – as friends. Then one day they meet a handsome man with gorgeous eyes. Suddenly they not only want him but want to have his children. These women either don't know about *The Rules* or have never practised them. This is why you should always do *The Rules*. You never know when you'll want to get married.

Another reason to do *The Rules* is so that people – men, women, bosses, parents – treat us well. When we don't do *The Rules*, we inevitably get hurt. When we do *The Rules*, we find out who really loves us. The answer might be painful, but better to weed out the uninterested parties than to carry on unsatisfying relationships. For example, you ask a man out and he says no, or he says yes to be polite and never calls again. You're hurt. But had you not initiated the date, he would never have hurt you. You have no one to blame but yourself! Or let's say your neighbour only comes by to borrow milk or when he's bored. You wish he would invite you to dinner. He doesn't. So you suggest dinner. He makes excuses. You're hurt. Again, situations of our own making! If someone is not asking you out, then they don't want to be with you. Go about your business and trust you will meet other people who genuinely like you and want to be with you. You might feel lonely and hurt for a while, but better that than being rejected.

The Rules can be used in many life situations and applied to other people (see also *Rule 55*). For example, if you love your sister too much, but she doesn't act particularly warm or nurturing toward you, don't call her every day. Just return her calls. Stop trying to 'work things out' or go over childhood feelings. Just get a life so that your relationship with her is not the main thing on your mind. Be busy and when she finally calls you, be friendly. No one likes talking to someone who is angry or depressed.

You may be thinking, 'But without so-and-so, I wouldn't have a friend to go to singles dinners with or a summer house to visit.' We know how you feel, but maybe you're supposed to go to dinners by yourself or you're supposed to let go of so-and-so to make room for better friends. Just do *The Rules*. Don't think about the short-term result. Trust that you will find other ways to fill the emptiness. Maybe you'll take up running and meet someone on the track. Looking back, whenever we did *The Rules* and lost a relationship, we got a better one.

You see, whenever you love someone more than that person loves you, you are in a position to get hurt. *The*

Rules way of thinking and acting protects you from unnecessary pain. It's a law of the universe that the more you try to get the love and attention of someone who doesn't naturally want you, the more frustrated and unhappy you will be. When we do *The Rules*, we give up the struggle. We accept that some people don't want us and we go on to the next. We don't force people to love us.

We had to change our definition of gratifying relationships. A gratifying relationship is long lasting and mutual, not short-term and hurtful!

When we do *The Rules* in life, whether or not we want to get married, we create boundaries with people. Some of us get so overly friendly with our secretary, babysitter, or cleaning lady that they take advantage of us and don't do their jobs. We should be friendly but always remain the boss. We say yes to last-minute dates or let men get off the phone first, and then we wonder why we feel so empty. At work, we try too hard to make our co-workers like us, but they sense our motives and find us annoying.

If you think of *The Rules* as a manual for life rather than simply as rules for getting married, you might do them more often. Then, when you meet the man of your dreams, you'll have had plenty of *Rules* practice.

Buyer Beware
(Weeding Out Mr Wrong)!

The Rules are not about marrying the first man you are attracted to who calls you by Wednesday for Saturday night and buys you flowers. It's about marrying your own personal Mr Right – a man whom you love and whose character you admire and can live with.

Love may be blind, but *Rules* girls are not stupid! In addition to doing *The Rules*, you should be observing his behaviour in various situations to decide if he's right for you. You may want to keep notes in a diary to keep track of what he says and how he acts in his relationship with you. For example, is he a man of his word or does he promise and not deliver? Does he speak badly about people or tell horrible stories about ex-girlfriends? Is he cheap on dates? Is he critical of you? Does he drink or smoke too much? Is he rude to waiters? If either of you has been married before, how does he treat his children or your children?

It's easy to ignore certain behaviour, but if it's written down in black and white, you will see a pattern emerge and not be able to lie to yourself or sweep it under the rug.

Don't marry thinking you will change this kind of

behaviour – people don't usually change that much. We believe that anything you don't like about the man you marry was there when you were dating him – you just didn't really think about it seriously or told yourself you didn't mind.

A woman we know who followed *The Rules* called us one day to say Mr Right had proposed. We were thrilled, but we quickly got suspicious when she told us that six months had passed and he still hadn't committed to a wedding date. She, too, felt something was wrong, but she really wanted to marry this man. We advised her to try to pin him down to a date. When she did, he admitted that he was back with his ex-girlfriend.

If something doesn't feel right to you about a man, it probably isn't! If you don't want to be miserable and full of regrets later on, you have to pay attention now. *Rules* girls don't sleep at the wheel!

No, *Rules* girls take a very active role in choosing Mr Right. At first glance, *The Rules* may seem like passive dating – let him call you, let him ask you out, let him pick you up, let him do all the work. In terms of the chase, that's certainly true. But we are also telling women to actively evaluate a man's character and behaviour. Did he call when he said he'd call? Did he remember your birthday?

A *Rules* girl is always carefully observing his behaviour and taking notes. This *is* active, not passive, dating.

When we told you to 'be quiet and mysterious, act

ladylike, cross your legs and smile and don't talk so much' on the first few dates, we did not mean that you shouldn't think! We told you this for two reasons:

(a) so you don't tell him your whole life story too soon and live to regret it, and equally important,

(b) so you *listen*. The less you talk, the more you can hear and pick up clues if he's right for you.

Sometimes a woman is so anxious to get married to a man she is attracted to – a man who is chasing her thanks to *The Rules* – that she blocks out traits she doesn't like about him. She hopes that love and marriage will change him in time. We say, maybe, maybe not. It's true that former playboy types lose interest in the club scene when they meet a *Rules* girl and become fond of changing diapers when they have a child. But we also say, what you see is what you get, so don't count on a man changing.

Let's look at some specific dilemmas you might be facing:

Dilemma #1: You're amazed – and impressed – by his sophistication with alcohol. He puts away countless gin and tonics without a problem, and you're charmed by the way he orders the best bottle of wine at romantic restaurants! But after reading this *Rule*, you remember that most of the time you had mineral water and *he* gladly drank the whole bottle.

Buyer beware: Love won't change and addiction and heavy drinking isn't charming when you have kids to support and he's throwing money away at bars, or you are the designated driver after every party. If you think he drinks too much, don't marry him unless he agrees to seek help and has stopped drinking for at least a year. It's good for him and it's good for you.

Dilemma #2: You think you've found Mr Right, except that he'd rather read the newspaper or work on the computer than have sex with you most week nights and even Sunday mornings. Now that you're reading this chapter, you remember that he was always a little too intellectual for your taste. You wished he were more passionate, not so cerebral.

Buyer beware: This will be a problem in your marriage if sex and passion are important to you.

Dilemma #3: He's very good looking, personable, and a ton of fun, but not as deep as you would like him to be. You are a serious reader – you tend to be analytical and you are into yoga and meditation. He likes action sports such as tennis and basketball. You want to have soulful discussions; he's more pragmatic.

Buyer beware: This will be a problem if you like to have philosophical conversations with your mate. Just know that he may ask you to have breakfast with him or play tennis when you're in the middle of yoga or meditation.

Dilemma #4: He's into a whirlwind courtship. He calls you day and night and proposes after a month or two. You think he's a little impulsive, but you're also thrilled!

Buyer beware: If you allow yourself to get caught up in a

whirlwind romance and move at his speed, you may live to regret it. You need to pace the relationship — to wait and allow yourself time to observe his behaviour in many different situations — before you make such a serious commitment. Otherwise, you may find out *after* you're married that he's a womaniser, gambler, emotionally immature, in deep financial debt or has a criminal past. By then it might be too late.

Dilemma #5: He's exciting and debonair, but he has a dark side. You've heard him scream at his family, his friends and even business associates.
Buyer beware: He may yell or be violent toward you or your children.

Dilemma #6: He loves you, but is often annoyed by close girlfriends, your family and any man who pays too much attention to you. He gets angry if you don't tell him everything or include him in everything.
Buyer beware: While it's flattering to be the centre of a man's attention, as opposed to being ignored, know that you might have fights about his level of involvement in your day-to-day activities.

Sometimes a problem is not his character, but circumstances, such as:

Dilemma #7: You love him, but he's much older than you, divorced and a devoted father to two teenagers. You never cared for children, much less stepchildren.

Buyer beware: You may resent his children and the time they take away from your relationship. You might also resent the amount of money he is paying to his ex-wife to support them.

Sometimes the problem is not him at all, but *you*. Your motives are not so good, such as:

Dilemma #8: You love him but, truth be told, you wouldn't be marrying him if he wasn't also rich.
Buyer beware: What are you going to do if his business sours and he no longer can buy you diamonds and fur coats? What if you actually have to go back to work?

In the above scenarios, we are not saying 'don't marry him'. We are simply saying go into the marriage with your eyes open. Be honest with yourself! Check your motives! *Rules* girls don't get married at any cost!

If you don't want to have problems later on, think twice about marrying for money or power, unless you can live with the downside. Think twice about marrying to get even with your ex-husband who left you for a younger woman or to escape a bad home life. Think twice about marrying anyone simply to have children.

And don't be lax about discussing major issues such as religion or whether to have children *before* you get married.

While making sure you are marrying Mr Right is not always so easy, by doing *The Rules* you at least weed out Mr Wrong.

For example, any man who is interested in you just

for sex, money, or convenience automatically loses interest because you are not sleeping with him right away, you are not supporting him, and you are not meeting him when and where it's convenient for him.

A man has to *really care about you* to call you early in the week (every week), make plans, pick you up and wait until you're ready to have sex! Mr Wrongs simply won't put up with the rigors of *The Rules* – they move on to women without such standards.

So while you're doing *The Rules*, you should also be observing, writing and thinking, *Is he the right one for me*? Take an active role – your long-term happiness is definitely worth the work.

Closing The Deal
(Getting Him to the Altar)

We're not talking about a business deal here, but getting the man you want to propose and then to turn that proposal into an actual wedding date – a feat some women would say can be tougher than any corporate transaction. Of course, it's made much easier by doing *The Rules*.

If you've been following *The Rules* from the moment you met Mr Right and he says he loves you, he *will* propose – sometimes in a matter of a few months, but usually within fifteen months. (He may have his own 'rules' about dating you for four seasons before proposing, and there's nothing wrong with that.)

By doing *The Rules* you will not only get a proposal, but you will know where the relationship is going long before he pops the question. You will sense a warm, open feeling emanating from him, a desire to include you in his world. Here are some of the key words and phrases he is likely to bring up in conversations with you:

1. The future – whether it be where he wants to live, his career goals or the car he is planning to buy.

2. Marriage (the *M*-word) – for example, he'll *volunteer* that he's going to be the best man when his friend gets married.
3. Kids – he might mention his nephew's upcoming birthday.
4. Married friends – he might discuss his married friends or suggest doubling with them.
5. His family – he'll talk about his parents and ask you about yours or invite you to a family gathering for the holidays.

He'll also include you in the most minute details of his day – i.e., he'll tell you that he got a haircut or he washed the car. He's always bringing you closer to him.

Because you let him pursue you, didn't see him more than two or three times a week, refused to go away with him on week-long holidays, have not moved in or crowded him in any way, you've actually helped him to fall in love with you and *want* to marry you. He wants more of you, not less.

Within a year, if not sooner, he's figured out that he not only *wants* to marry you but *has* to marry you to see you more often, to really have you.

Your problem is not *if* he's going to marry you, but when. Men can date for five years! They are notorious for wanting to put off the actual engagement part until later. If he suggests living together first to see if you get along or to see you more often, tell him you're old-fashioned and want to wait until you're engaged or married.

A man can love you, but marriage ... that's a little scary. Maybe he's just trying to hold on to his bachelorhood, maybe he's been married before and isn't in any rush to do it again, or maybe he's young (under twenty-five years old).

In general, the way to get a man to ask you to marry him in a reasonable amount of time is not to live with him before you're engaged or married and to continue to see him only three times a week, even though by this time you want to be inseparable.

If that doesn't work, you might have to shake things up a little bit – go away for a weekend with a girlfriend, cancel a Saturday night date, get very busy at work, mention that you are renewing your flat lease, and be mysterious about your activities. All of the above should make him anxious to propose. As you already know, a man who is wary of commitment is made less wary by a woman moving *away* from, not *toward*, commitment. This isn't trickery. You're just giving him space.

On the other hand, if you have not done *The Rules* all along, getting a man to propose can be very difficult.

If you have been dating a man for two, three or even five years and he has not proposed, you might be thinking that if you hang around long enough, he will eventually ask. You have probably accepted his excuses – financial problems, married before, not ready and so on – as to why he can't marry you just yet. But now that you've read *The Rules*, you know that a *Rules* girl doesn't date a man forever and the way to get him to propose (if he's going to propose at all) is *not* to hang around.

Let's say you've been dating him for more than a year and he's somehow avoided the whole issue of marriage and the future, what should you do?

Ask him his intentions. If he says he has no plans to marry you, say 'Okay' and then never see him again. Men don't lie about things like this. He's not scared of commitment – he doesn't want to marry you.

If he says he does plan to marry you some day, then it's up to you to *close the deal*. Ask him when and if it's more than a year, see less of him and think about dating others. You've already spent more than a year waiting for him to propose, do you have another year to wait?

If you are already living together (because you found out about *The Rules* after you moved in) and he says he doesn't want to get engaged, make plans to move out. But don't say, 'I'm moving out because you won't commit.' That would be too obvious. Just say you need more space and that you heard about a great flat or your friend is renting hers. When a man doesn't want to commit, we leave him alone. If he doesn't try to stop you or get you back with a proposal, don't waste your time. If he asks what's going on, nonchalantly answer, 'I don't know if this relationship is for me.' If he can live without you, you don't want him. You move on.

Here are five things *not* to do, no matter how tempting:

1. Don't tell him you're hurt, mad or reprimand him for wasting your time or leading you on. You lived with him – no one twisted your arm. Take responsibility for your actions. By not doing *The Rules*, you

199

allowed him to be with you indefinitely. In a *Rules* relationship a man either proposes within a year – two years at the max! – or it's *next*!

2. Don't suggest going to couples therapy to discuss why *he* can't commit. Men can and do commit when they love you and you do *The Rules* on them. But they can become 'commitment phobic' when a woman has pursued them, is too available or they're just not in love with her. They say things like, 'I find marriage a difficult concept to swallow,' or they conveniently cite the high divorce rate.

3. Don't let a man brainwash you into thinking that marriage isn't important – 'just a piece of paper' – and that as long as you're together that's all that matters. If he doesn't want to marry you then he's not *that* in love with you or it's not the brand of love you want. What it really means is he still wants the option of meeting someone else!

4. Don't let a man convince you that because he's been married before he can't marry you or that you should give him time to recover from Wife No. 1 or 2.

5. Don't let a man you have been dating for years convince you to wait until 'things slow down' at work or he's better off financially to make a commitment. This is the worst reason. There will always be work/money issues in life. They should have nothing to do with marrying you. When a man loves you and wants to marry you he hopes you don't notice these issues, or he includes you in their solutions and begs you to marry him anyway. He

gets down on one bended knee and says something like, 'Look, I know I'm not a millionaire, but I love you and I'd do anything for you'. When a man says 'You're too good for me', what he really means is 'I don't want you.'

In conclusion, the same man who won't commit because of issues with his ex-wife or his finances has no problem proposing to a woman who refused to date him longer than a year. Sometimes a man will date a woman for five years claiming he has commitment issues and after breaking up with her, easily marries someone else in six months.

If you are involved with a man for several years who isn't proposing, how much longer are you willing to wait? When a man knows that you will accept less than marriage he is not motivated to fully commit himself. You must be willing to walk away from a dead-end relationship.

Assuming you are engaged, how do you get him to walk down the aisle?

The truth is, if you're engaged as a result of *The Rules*, getting him to marry you should not be a problem. There's no 'cold feet' in *Rules* engagements. In fact, just the opposite is the case. He's made his decision, he wants to get married, to be with you all the time, forever.

There's usually a wondrous, exciting planning of the wedding. He's calling caterers, videographers, and tuxedo places, and driving himself crazy trying to pick the most meaningful wedding song. He's intimately involved in every detail of the wedding. He's worried that you might not get your dress in time. The only time he is angry at you is when you're not making the wedding your top priority.

Of course, getting engaged is no *guarantee* of marriage, so don't get lax about *The Rules* when you're engaged. Don't think you can talk to him on the phone for hours, and it's still best not to move in together yet. Engagements can be broken and wedding dates postponed or never set. If you move in, he may change his mind and decide not to marry you so soon! Better that he miss you and move up the wedding date than feel claustrophobic as you take over his wardrobe space.

Also, be on the alert for any special circumstances or excuses your fiancé might make, such as:

1. He thinks being engaged is great, but why rush marriage?
2. He's been married before, it was a disaster and he's not anxious to tie the knot again. He gave you the ring so he doesn't lose you (so you won't sleep with anyone else), but he's happy with the status quo.
3. He's young and still likes to go out with his friends, not be tied down. He likes the bachelor life and although you convinced him to get engaged, you can't pin him down for a wedding date. You have a ring but you're not sure what the future looks like.
4. You were already living together when you got

engaged, but you still don't have a wedding date set. What to do?

In general, we feel that when you get engaged you should set a wedding date. *Rules* engagements are usually a year or less. If you're young (under twenty-five), a two-year engagement is fine.

If the engagement is dragging on, you may want to think about giving him back the ring and moving on. Perhaps he's not Mr Right. *Rules* girls don't waste time.

Not Closing the Deal (Being True to Yourself): Perhaps you're the one having second thoughts. You did *The Rules*, he may or may not have proposed, but now you're having doubts about him and the relationship. Something just doesn't feel right, you're thinking about breaking it off. Perhaps you're finding out that he's not the man of your dreams after all, or there are just extenuating circumstances. What should you do?

If you've thought about it carefully and discussed your decision with a therapist, good friends or family members, we suggest you always trust your instincts. *Do Not Close the Deal*.

Don't feel silly, embarrassed, or guilty. Don't hate yourself or feel like a failure or that you wasted a year or two of your life. You didn't. Ending a relationship that isn't right is a learning and growing experience. Besides, you're not the first woman to change her mind or cancel a wedding. It happens sometimes. You tried, it didn't work out, much better to find out and disentangle yourself now than later on. Don't stay with him because you're a couple, you've made future plans together, you like his parents, you're entrenched and it feels complicated to break it off at this stage of the game.

After you've made up your mind, give yourself time and permission to cry and grieve. Who wouldn't be upset? It's normal. But don't give up on love or throw yourself in front of a bus. Keep the faith. Always remember, there's another person out there — the real Mr Right — for you and you're a winner for being honest with yourself! Pump yourself up by rereading *The Rules*, specifically *Rule 1: Be a 'Creature Unlike Any Other'*. You trust in the abundance and goodness of the universe: if not him, someone better ... Any man would be lucky to have you! Plan a social action, get back on track! Keep doing *The Rules*. Your *real* Mr Right may be just around the corner and when you meet him you won't regret past break-ups!

Even if You're Engaged or Married, You Still Need *The Rules*

Ideally, we do *The Rules* from the minute we meet a man until he says he loves us and proposes. But if you were not lucky enough to learn about *The Rules* before reading this book, we suggest you do the best you can right now. Better to do *The Rules* now than not at all.

However, if you did not know about *The Rules* until now, don't think you can totally erase the way you related to your fiancé or husband from the beginning of courtship. For example, if you initiated the relation-ship, called him up, asked him out and so on, in order to make the relationship work, he'll always expect such things from you. He didn't worry about getting you to marry him, he knew he had you, you told him so with every word and gesture, so on some level he may take you for granted. And chances are you still make things happen by initiating sex and/or romantic dinners, asking him about his feelings for you, wishing he would spend less time in the office or with his friends and more time with you. You might even wonder from time to time if he's having an affair.

If you didn't do *The Rules* at the beginning of your relationship, your husband might ignore you, talk to you rudely or treat you badly. You might wonder, 'Is his behaviour the result of bad upbringing or something in his past?' Maybe. But we believe it's because you didn't do *The Rules*. He never needed to treat you like his dream girl. The same man who would act indifferent or ignore a wife who pursued him wouldn't dream of it with the woman who did *The Rules*.

Abuse doesn't happen in a *Rules* relationship because when you play hard to get and he works like hell to get you, he thinks you're the most beautiful, wonderful woman in the world, even if you're not. He treats you like a precious jewel.

But don't despair. Start doing *The Rules* now as best you can and he may notice a difference in your behaviour and want you more. Here are five suggestions:

1. Don't call him at work so often. When you do keep it brief and practical ('What time is the film on?'). Don't call saying, 'I miss you. Let's make love tonight.' He should be calling you to express those sentiments.

2. Don't initiate sex, even if you want it badly. Let him be the man, the aggressor in the bedroom. Biologically, the man must pursue the woman. If you bring up sex all the time, you will emasculate him. Act as if you're a *Rules* girl on a first date. Be coy. Flirt when he tries to kiss you or bite your neck. This will turn him into a tiger.

3. Dress better, a little sexier. No man likes coming home to a woman wearing sweatpants or a

bathrobe all the time. Try wearing tight jeans, a miniskirt or a deep V-necked shirt in a bright colour. Put on some makeup and perfume. Wash your hair. Pretend you're dating him.

4. Act independent. Always be *coming* or *going*. Don't sit on the couch waiting for him to come home. Don't bore him with details about your day or your aches and pains. Make lots of plans with friends, your kids, the neighbours. Go to the movies, go shopping. Just go. This will make him desperate to catch a minute of your time. He will want to corner you in the kitchen for a kiss if he senses you're not around much. He'll get mad if you're on the phone when he's home because he'll want you all to himself. This is how it is when you do *The Rules*. He'll feel as if he can never get enough of you. He'll start calling you from work to suggest dinners alone or a weekend getaway. This is what you want. Men love independent women because they leave them alone. They love chasing women who are busy. It gives them a thrill, as big as scoring a goal.

5. Take up a hobby. Most men are content to sit around in a recliner on a Saturday afternoon and drink beer and watch football. Some bring work home from the office and spend the entire afternoon on the computer. Women tend to feel empty when their boyfriends or husbands don't include them in their plans or pay attention to them. It's imperative that you don't nag him to give up his hobbies, friends or work because you're bored.

You'll get more attention from him if you get even busier than he is. Make play dates for the kids, go out for a run or take an aerobics class at a gym. That will not only keep you busy but also will get you in shape, making you all that more attractive to him. He may wonder if other men are looking at you in your Lycra. That will be good for the relationship. It will make him want to turn off the TV or computer and be alone with you. You might get involved in charity, read a book, take up a sport. The key here is to keep yourself independent and busy. This way you're not hanging around him complaining that he's not paying enough attention to you!

Unfortunately, doing *The Rules* sometimes means acting single (even if you're married with children) all over again. Just be grateful you're not!

Rules For The Bedroom
(When You're Married)

If you want to have a happy marriage, remember to make time for your sex life! You played hard to get, you got him, now make the effort to maintain a healthy sex life with him.

Make your sex life a priority, even if you had a long day at work or your kids were unusually demanding and sex is the last thing on your mind. Or, you may be having one of those superbly, bad hair days. You don't think you look very sexy and sure don't *feel* sexy. Okay, every woman has days like that. We say, try to make the time and be loving anyway!

In addition, be realistic about sex. You may want your time together to be just right – unhurried and romantic. That's not always possible – so try to be flexible. Sometimes sex is the culmination of a beautiful, enchanted evening. At other times, you just seize the opportunity – i.e., in the morning before the kids get up.

You may have a lot on your mind. You're thinking about your sales presentation due the next morning, your kids, how the house needs straightening, and so on. *Let it go*. We all have thoughts whirling in our brains. You don't always have to have an uncluttered mind to have sex. Sometimes sex can unclutter it!

Some women use sex as a bargaining tool. This is a bad idea. If you are trying to make a point, use a different method to get your message across. Don't make his favourite pasta or go with him to the football game. It's not healthy for your relationship to use sex as a weapon, as a way to hurt him. Remember, he can go to the football game with one of his friends, but when it comes to sex, you're the only one!

Of course, if you *do* have the time and the energy, may we suggest you make sex extra special by creating a romantic evening? Take the silver candlestick holders you received as a wedding present out of the cupboard and cook his favourite dinner, play some soft music, wear his favourite outfit and be loving. Once in a while, you could ask your parents or in-laws to watch the kids and plan a romantic weekend getaway.

You'll be happier – in the long run – if you have a healthy sex life! Here are seven reasons why:

1. It will help keep your commitment to each other strong!
2. He'll think about you more often during the day.
3. He'll appreciate your thoughtfulness.
4. He'll be less likely to stay late at the office.
5. He'll always want to be with you or call you.
6. He won't be so grouchy. (Big smile.)
7. You won't be so grouchy. (Even bigger smile).

Always be pleased and flattered because your husband wants to have sex with you. In a *Rules* marriage, your husband comes to you for sex and you're both happy.

Rules for Same-Sex Relationships

Do *The Rules* apply to same-sex relationships? If so, how? Do both people do *The Rules*? Or one? Which one?

Confused? Don't be. It's really quite simple. It's a self-diagnosable problem.

Everyone who is gay or lesbian knows whether or not they are the kind of person who needs structure, some sort of self-protection, in a relationship. If you are this type of person, you're probably very sensitive. You think a lot – obsessively may be more accurate – about the other person and the relationship. You get down – really down – when overlooked or rejected. You're not the type who naturally moves on. You don't think break-ups are for the best. You think they are downright devastating!

Perhaps you've been hurt before, or experienced a life-time of hurts, not to mention the social pressures that go alone with being gay. You want to be in a loving relationship, but you can't bear getting hurt again. Then *The Rules* are for you.

Much of the focus on gay issues has been on coming to recognize and accept one's individual sexual identity, not on how to *behave* in same-sex relationships. Here we attempt to fill that void with some sound advice.

The Rules can work like a charm when used by individuals who want to know the 'how to' of dating when they are completely at ease with their sexuality but at an emotional roadblock as to how to proceed. Do you ask someone out or wait to be asked? Should you play hard to get?

Don't think there aren't any rules. There are, it's just that there's a little more camaraderie and mutuality in same-sex relationships than in male-female relationships. You can show some interest, you can return some phone calls. It's not so one-sided. There's more balance.

When you go out to places alone or with friends, you're open to meeting someone, you're just not desperate. You don't aggressively approach anyone at a party. You smile back if someone smiles at you, and if someone moves a little closer to you, you give a 'It's okay to move in closer' smile. You want to let the person know you're approachable, that you are open to the idea of meeting someone. But that's all.

Eventually a conversation begins. It's going well. You're both animated. You laugh, at the room, at the night, at the jokes, but you don't bare your soul, your feelings. You're light-hearted. You come on slow, not like gang-busters. *You're not too much, too soon.*

Being gay or lesbian, perhaps you've felt a little isolated or separate your whole life. You've been waiting to meet someone who 'understands'. But when you do actually meet someone special, don't reveal too much – find a good friend or therapist to share your intimate problems with. Don't unload all of your past history on a new person for they will probably be overwhelmed by your intensity. Worse, they may be very happy to have you depend so much on them, but it will create the kind of co-dependent, needy relationship you *don't* want.

It is very hard to keep from sharing too much when you find someone who is receptive. After all, there aren't a lot of people who understand what you have had to go through. But motivate yourself to use restraint with the knowledge that you are building a solid relationship and sparing yourself the pain that accompanies the inevitable end of an overly dependent one.

So, be casual. The person must give you signs that they would like to get together again. You will get a *feeling*. It's different from a male–female relationship because if the man doesn't ask the woman out, that's it, it's over. In same-sex relationships, the lines are a little more blurry, but rules still exist, and following them is not as hard as you think.

Pace the relationship. Get to know the person you're interested in slowly – don't spill all the beans during a three-hour coffee date. You are drawn to the person, but you don't bare all. Wait as long as you can, knowing that the more mysterious you are, the better.

The idea is to bring the *spirit* of *The Rules* into your dating life. You should *never* pursue anyone relentlessly. If there's no mutual interest, no give and take, then there's nothing. If the person you're involved with seems to enjoy being the pursuer, that's great and actually makes things easier. You enjoy being pursued and you're sure of their feelings for you so you're less anxious.

Regardless, don't stay on the phone for hours and don't see the person at a moment's notice. You have a life, you have other plans, you are not waiting to be rescued.

Don't feel pressured to have sex right away. Don't see this person all the time or live together until you're exclusive.

Maintain your self-esteem and self-respect. If the other person has a wandering eye, neglects you, or constantly makes sexual comments about other people when you're around, move on to new possibilities.

You know that a relationship without boundaries, without give and take, is not a relationship that is worth having. Perhaps you've settled before. Now, armed with *The Rules*, you don't want anything less than lasting, secure love. You want the best. You deserve the best, and by following *The Rules*, you will get the best!

Next! And Other *Rules* for
Dealing with Rejection

Life is not always fair. Fortunately, *The Rules* will help ensure that you are never unnecessarily hurt by a man. By behaving around men in a *Rules* way – independent and busy, not needy or aggressive – we do not put ourselves in a position to be hurt.

However, we cannot make a certain man like us or prevent a man from meeting someone else he likes better and consequently dropping us. And we can't stop an ex-girlfriend from winning him back. So what do we do when we get dumped?

Our natural reaction may be to stagnate and isolate, wish we were dead, not wash our hair or wear makeup, cry, sleep a lot, play sad love songs and swear we'll never meet anyone as perfect as him again. We might find consolation in the refrigerator or talk non-stop about him to our friends. Obviously, this is ridiculous. Allow yourself about two days of such behaviour and then go on.

The Rules recipe for rejection is to wear a great dress and flattering makeup and go to the *very* next party or singles dance and tell your friends you're available for blind dates. Hopefully, you've been diligent about *The*

Rules up to the break-up and your social calendar is already full of dates. Remember, until the ring is on your finger or you're exclusive – by exclusive, we mean he's serious about marrying you and it's just a matter of time before he pops the question, as opposed to he's dating you until someone better comes along – you should be dating others. Nothing is better for cushioning the blow than the adoring attention of other men.

Whatever you do, don't lose your cool over this man. Now is the time to acquire faith, to believe in abundance. Tell yourself he is not the last man on earth, there are many others and certainly at least one out there for you. Talk to women friends who were dumped and then met 'The One'. They will tell you how happy they are now that so-and-so broke up with them, even though they didn't realize it at the time. Comfort yourself with uplifting slogans like, 'When one door closes, another one opens' and any other positive philosophies you can think of.

Remember, *Rules* girls don't get hung up on men who reject them. They say, 'His loss' or '*Next*!' They carry on. They don't tear themselves apart and wish they had done this differently or said this and not that. They don't write men letters offering to change or make things work out. They don't call them or send messages via friends. They accept it's over and get on with it. They don't waste time.

Do *The Rules*, Even When Your Friends and Parents Think It's Nuts

Remember your reaction when you first heard about *The Rules* or read this book? No doubt you thought the idea was crazy, dishonest or extreme. 'Why can't love be more natural? Why can't I ask a man out? After all, this is the 21st century.' But because your way didn't work, you became open-minded rather quickly. Something deep down inside you said *The Rules* just might be the answer.

Well, don't be surprised if the people around you don't support your new philosophy. Don't be surprised if they think you're nuts or question every move you make or don't make. When a man you're dating calls and leaves a message with your mother, don't be surprised if she hovers over you like a bee nagging you to call him back right away. Rather than say, 'I can't call him back. I'm doing *The Rules*', just say, 'Okay, mum, later, after I wash my hair.' Keep postponing any *Rule*-breaking activity.

Your mother may hassle you, but it's your girlfriends that will probably give you the hardest time, possibly because they're not doing *The Rules* themselves. Don't be surprised if they take your devotion to *The Rules* as antifeminist. They may ask things like, 'You know, marriage isn't the answer. No man is going to fix you. There has to be a "me" before a "we". You don't need *The Rules*. You need some good analysis to find out why you want to get married so much!' Don't say, 'If I don't get married I'm going to kill myself' or 'In Noah's ark, they went in twos.' Just smile and change the subject.

Your friends might tell you that *The Rules* are dishonest, that you should let a man know exactly who you are, that it's rude not to call him or call him back. Unless they want to do *The Rules* themselves, don't argue with them or explain what you are doing. Just do *The Rules* quietly and let the results speak for themselves. The fact is that your friends and others might not have that burning desire to get married and have babies. They may be perfectly content in their careers and hobbies. You, on the other hand can't imagine life without a husband. Neither could we. That's why we did *The Rules* – to ensure that the right man didn't get away.

We suggest you find like-minded women who believe in *The Rules*, want to get married and support each other much like any support group. Call *them* when you want to call him. Don't bother asking your male friends if they like being pursued by women. They might say one thing and believe another. They will probably tell you that they're flattered to be called and asked out by women. What they won't say is that these are not the women they end up marrying or even dating.

Don't take a poll of men, or of married people for that matter. Your married friends or relatives might tell you, 'I didn't do *The Rules* and I got married.' They will poke holes into every rule, one telling you that she asked him out for the second date, and the other that she paid for the third dinner date. Don't argue with these people. Don't tell them you're doing *The Rules* because nothing else has worked. Just smile and say, 'Oh, it's just for fun' and change the subject. Don't stop doing *The Rules* because married women tell you they didn't. How do you know what their marriage is like? How do you know that, because she pursued him, he isn't always neglecting her or spending too much time at the office? You want a *Rules* marriage, not just any marriage.

If you can't find any like-minded women to support you in doing *The Rules*, just read this book a lot, carry it around in your bag to refer to on long supermarket lines, and practise what you read as much as possible. Believe us, if you do *The Rules*, you'll be so busy dating your future husband to care or even think about what anyone else is doing or what anyone else thinks of what you are doing.

Keep Doing *The Rules*
Even When Things Are Slow

A very important *Rules* credo is that it's better to date no one than to date or marry Mr Wrong. Better to spend Saturday night baby-sitting or curled up with a good book than with a man who's not in love with you.

Let's say you've been doing *The Rules* for six months or even a year, but have nothing to show for it. No husband, no steady boyfriend, and few Saturday night dates. You go to parties, museums and singles events, you look good, and you don't pursue men. Men you're attracted to don't approach you and the ones you don't care about won't leave you alone! Meanwhile, your friends who aren't doing *The Rules* seem to be dating all the time. True, their relationships aren't good – sometimes downright bad! – and don't last, but at least they're busy and you're all alone. Even your mother is telling you to call men! What's wrong with this picture?

Unfortunately, nothing. You just haven't met Mr Right yet. The fact is, Mr Right – the man you want to marry who wants and pursues you – only comes around a few times in a lifetime. So don't be surprised if you come home from parties with nothing good to report other than that you did *The Rules*. You didn't meet anyone. No man asked you for your number.

Many women we know went through the nothing-to-show-for-it period for a year or so, but now are happily married. They didn't weaken and stop doing *The Rules*.

Don't be surprised if you're tempted to break *The Rules* during these dead periods. You might long to initiate a conversation with the first cute guy you see or call an old boyfriend who didn't treat you well in an attempt to rekindle something dead and buried, just out of boredom and loneliness. We understand how you feel, but don't give in! You're just asking for heartache and wasting your time.

Realize that these dead periods are not dead at all. *The Rules* are actually working in your life because you are weeding out unsuitable men, which is just as important as holding out for Mr Right.

When you feel that nothing is happening in the man area, take advantage of this down time and pursue that MBA or law degree, finish the novel you started writing in college, redecorate or find a hobby. Take up tennis or diving. Don't forget to call *Rules*-minded women for reinforcement. Anything – but don't initiate a relationship with a man who isn't right for you. You never know – you might just meet your husband on the tennis court or your adult education class.

Women who break *The Rules* when nothing is going on end up in relationships that don't work out and, even worse, get involved in relationships that prevent them from meeting Mr Right. Five months or five years later, they're still single. *Rules* girls don't waste time!

Don't Break *The Rules*

If you break *The Rules*, will he still marry you?

Women are always asking us this question. They do *The Rules* for a month or two and then stop. He still hasn't said 'I love you,' much less proposed; yet, these women are now asking him out, bringing up marriage, and in some cases cleaning and decorating his apartment. They don't realize that *The Rules* way is not a hobby, but a religion. We keep doing *The Rules* until the ring is on our finger!

Let's take the case of our good friend, Candy. We told her about *The Rules* and she admitted she pursued men and they never proposed. She finally became willing to do everything we suggested for the first month or so of dating a hard catch named Barry. *The Rules* worked so well for Candy that after two months Barry took her to Jamaica for a week. That's when Candy went back to her old ways, ignoring our suggestions. She didn't think she had to do them anymore!

During their holiday, Candy asked for assurances about their future and acted more amorously than he did by leaving love poetry on his pillow and initiating sex. When they returned to New York and continued dating, she suggested they get together during the week as well as on weekends. Whenever he kissed her good night, she suggested they have sex or rent a video or do some other thing to prolong their time together. He finally told her, 'I love you, but I'm not *in* love with you. It's really strange because in the beginning there was something about you I had to get to know, but then it changed for me.' Sure, all that love poetry!

Candy had the strength to end the relationship shortly after he told her he didn't love her and didn't want to marry her. Men don't lie! When they say they are not in love, they mean it. They are giving you a hint to break it off and look elsewhere. Which most women don't heed. More often than not a woman will stay put, wasting precious time and hoping against hope that a man will change his mind. Have you ever gone through this? Aren't you tired of the pain? After Candy and Barry finally broke up, she *never* broke *The Rules* again. We are happy to report that she recently got married by doing *The Rules* as they are written, which should give all women hope, as many women break *The Rules* before they finally do them!

Rules girls don't hang around where they are not wanted. They don't try to revive a love gone sour. If you've broken *The Rules* to the point where he's convinced he's out of love with you, don't stick around hoping for a second chance. Remember, sometimes distance and time can make a man realize he's made the biggest mistake of his life. He can always call you – he has your phone number! Your part is to move on.

Better that you do *The Rules* perfectly in your next relationship than to hang around, tolerating the loveless feelings of your current flame. So the answer to the question, 'Will he still marry me if I break *The Rules*?' is, sorry to say, 'Maybe yes, but most likely, no.' So why take a chance?

That's why we strongly suggest that you don't break *The Rules* at all. Of course, you might make mistakes as you practise them. If you have chased men your whole life, you can consider it progress if you stop writing men love letters but call them once in a while. However, we believe in striving for perfection. When you do *The Rules* perfectly, you don't have to worry about second chances because he won't fall out of love with you. When you break *The Rules*, you automatically take away the pleasure men get from pursuing you, and they end up resenting you for it. Then they treat you badly and you're left wondering if it was something you said, did, didn't say or didn't do that caused the problem. The answer is simple: you broke *The Rules*.

Prepare yourself for the fact that you will usually want to break *The Rules* after you have been dating someone for a couple of months. You may feel that the relationship is slowing down or going nowhere. He starts calling less often or still hasn't brought up marriage. Your girlfriends are planning the wedding and you still haven't met his parents. You feel anxious. Naturally, you want to shake things up or move things along. You are tempted to send him heavy-handed greeting cards from the 'relationship' section of the card store or a love letter telling him how much you care about him to bring him closer to you. Without his permission, you want to throw out his old leather jacket and buy him a new one. You act as if you are his wife and feel entitled – after all, he sees you every weekend and bought you flowers twice. You may even decide to try and patch things up between him and his dad, who haven't spoken for a while. Let's face it, you are out of control!

Persist in this kind of behaviour only if you want to destroy any chance of his proposing! *The Rules* action to take when things slow down is more of the same: reread how to behave on the first few dates (see *Rules 10* and *11*). *Just hang out*, trust in the process, be patient, don't nag him and don't make anything happen. If you still feel frustrated after a few weeks, then get moving yourself! Rent that summer house with your girlfriend rather than waiting for him to suggest plans, or sign up for tennis lessons with that new instructor at your health club. Don't hone in on the man you are dating – he will feel smothered, not loved. Move away, get busy and elusive and he will either miss you or not. Best to find out now rather than later if he can live without you.

There are many ways to break *The Rules* in the early stages of a relationship. Here's another example:

After dating Ken for a month, Nicole decided to discard *The Rules*, which she had followed faithfully on the first four dates, and do what she felt like doing. If Ken was going to be her husband and father her children one day, she reasoned, why shouldn't she show him her true self? (Have you ever thought like Nicole?) So, for his birthday, she planned a big surprise party, partly as a ploy to meet his family and friends.

Not a weekend went by that Nicole's feelings didn't get the best of her. Once they passed a playground, she suggested that they ride on the seesaw and swing on the swings, hoping to make him think about children. Ken found her behaviour obvious and boring. The relationship went downhill from there. Nicole suggested couples therapy. He decided to break up with her and find someone else to date.

The lesson here is simple: don't break *The Rules*.

Don't make him a birthday party or give him an expensive gift, don't mention children, don't patch things up with his family, don't ask him out and try not to call him very often. Basically, don't push yourself into his life or you won't be his wife!

When we pursue a man, a bell goes off in his head. *The challenge is over* and his feelings start to fade. Suddenly, the romance turns to mud. Whatever he found adorable about you, he now finds annoying. You're no longer his dream girl. It's as if you picked up the bill or opened the door for him. You've taken his job away, you've done him a disservice.

So when you think that not calling him and other *Rules* are rude and hurtful, remember you are in fact helping him want you more. *The Rules* are actually *good* for him. So don't go by your feelings, just do *The Rules*.

The good news is that when a man is in love with you, he is not afraid to make a fool of himself by calling you five times in one day to tell you little, stupid things. (Yes, *he* can call you five times a day, but you can't or he'll think you're crazy!) You don't need to call him five times a day because when you do *The Rules* you have peace of mind. You don't need to call him for reassurance about the relationship because you're secure. And you don't have to stay up until 2 a.m. making excuses about why he hasn't called in two weeks because when you do *The Rules*, he calls every week, sometimes every day!

Rules girls don't fret too much. They do *The Rules* and, in return, men give them that secure, snug feeling of being loved and being asked out for Saturday night early in the week or, better yet, at the end of their last date.

Now we all know women who broke *The Rules* and got married anyway. We know one *Rule*-breaker who is always initiating intimacy with her husband. He says he loves her, but he never pinches her bottom in the kitchen and would rather watch the 11 o'clock news alone in his reclining chair than cuddle in bed with his wife.

So if you break *The Rules*, at least muster the courage to end the relationship when he says he is not in love and it's over. It will save you a lot of time. It's a spiritual axiom that when you feel someone slipping away, let the person go. Don't try to find out why he doesn't love you or what you could have done better. That's begging and, frankly, it's beneath a *Rules* girl to do. Be firm when it's over, knowing that you'll be able to break down and cry with your girlfriends later.

Even if you think you could have done *The Rules* better, don't blame yourself. Just love yourself and do them better the next time. Don't call him, don't talk to his friends about it, don't try to be buddies. It's over. *Next!* The relationship was not meant to be. There is somebody better out there for you. In the meantime, lining up a few dates is the best thing to do (and the best revenge).

Don't Worry, Even Men
Like *The Rules*

In case you forgot, you're doing *The Rules* because it's good for you and your self-esteem. Whether men like or dislike *The Rules* is irrelevant. The truth is, men can talk about wanting to date in an open, up-front, rational way, but what they respond to is altogether different — they respond to challenge, mystery and intrigue. If a man likes a woman, he'll call her again. If he likes her and she doesn't let the first date become a marathon, he'll want to see her again that much sooner. He'll lose interest if she breaks rules, regardless of *what he says!*

But you are probably curious what men think and say about *The Rules* anyway. We have found that, if presented correctly, most men don't find *The Rules* objectionable at all. They actually like the results *The Rules* produce.

Here is what men have told us in their own words:

'If I met a woman and thought she was "The One", I wouldn't let any book she was studying get in the way (of pursuing her),' says an executive at a university in New York.

He believes that men feel 'cheated' of the chase and 'refuse to commit' or demand 'space' when women break rules.

He is not alone. We have received dozens of letters and calls from men thanking us for writing *The Rules* and letting us know that they are buying copies for their daughters, sisters, female friends and ex-girlfriends.

A teacher from Lexington, Kentucky, wrote to say that he loved our description of a *Rules* girl – 'busy, with high self-esteem, not sleeping around or chasing married men, having values and ethics, and loving with her head and her heart. That is a very attractive woman to any sane man ...'

An M.D. from Chicago, Illinois, wrote to say that he was 'always getting into relationships with co-dependent women who had no lives of their own. These women were unusually clingy and bordering on being fatal attractions. Now, I have a renewed sense of hope in finding a woman who possesses the qualities of a *Rules* girl.'

Yet another male *Rules* fan from Los Angeles wrote, 'You are right – it is more exciting for us men when the girl is hard to get. I have never been interested in any girl who chased me. Flattered yes, but not interested.'

An Illinois medical student who is planning a career in psychiatry wrote, 'in my opinion, any young woman who knows and uses *The Rules* correctly will have a tremendous advantage in finding and keeping successful long-term relationships.'

Of course, there are men who think *The Rules* are just

silly – not offensive, just silly! These men simply cannot believe women read such books. But they don't realize the extent to which women can obsess about relationships. If a man actually knew how much a woman thought about him, a relationship gone wrong, or lost herself over a break-up with a man, he would really encourage her to do *The Rules*. He'd say, 'Well, go ahead then, read that book if it helps!'

So even if your boyfriend suspects you're doing *The Rules*, even if you think he'd be mad if he found out about it – so that's why you don't call me! – still do *The Rules*. Don't talk about it. Deep down, a man would rather you do *The Rules* than not, *no matter what they say*. Deep down, every man would rather marry a girl who gives him space and lets him breathe. So don't worry about what men think about *The Rules*, just do them. Men *do* like *Rules* girls – in fact, they do more than like them – they love and marry them!

Do *The Rules* and You'll Live Happily Ever After!

What can you expect to get when you do *The Rules*? The answer is total adoration from the man of your dreams. Otherwise, why else would we do them?

Let's face it, many of the things we ask you to do or not do in this book are downright difficult. Not calling him, not being intimate too soon, not bringing up marriage or children and ending the date first require a great deal of self-restraint, patience and determination. Sometimes we thought we would simply die at the thought of holding off having sex. And the agony of not calling him! There were many days when we just had to hear his voice.

So what kept us going? What made us continue doing *The Rules*? The incredible, unbelievable pay offs, twenty of which are listed below. So when you find yourself resisting doing a certain *Rule* (maybe you don't want to end the phone call after five or ten minutes because you're afraid he'll think you're rude and never call again), read this list and summon the courage. Remember, men want you more when you do *The Rules* and lose interest quicker when you don't!

1. The biggest payoff first: he wants to marry you! Most women bring up marriage or the future after a couple of weeks or months of dating a man. They want to know where the relationship is going. Most likely, it's going nowhere because men don't want to be pushed into proposing. As a *Rules* girl, you've been trained not to bring up marriage or kids. You talk about books, business, politics, football and the weather. When you do *The Rules*, he ends up proposing.

2. When you are seated at a booth in a restaurant, he slides over and sits next to you. Sitting opposite you is just *too far away* when he's truly in love.

3. He sends you roses after you have sex.

4. He writes love notes or poetry for you and tapes them on the refrigerator door.

5. He finds your idiosyncrasies harmless rather than annoying. You never have to worry that he'll leave you if you don't change a bad habit. He doesn't like it – but he doesn't leave you because of it.

6. He calls to see how your doctor's visit went.

7. He gives you little presents, jewellery and flowers on every possible occasion.

8. He gets angry when you don't pay attention to him. He wants your constant attention and companionship. He doesn't ignore you. He's always walking into whatever room you're in. You are never a 'football widow'. He wants to take you to the football game (even if you don't like the sport or understand it) in order to spend more time with you. He wants to do everything with you!

9. He is always ready to make up after a fight.
10. He gets involved in every aspect of your life. You don't bore him.
11. If you call him at work, he'll always want to talk to you even if he is busy. He calls you from work a lot anyway.
12. He doesn't like to work late because he wants to see more of you.
13. When you have a cold or become ill, he still wants to be with you.
14. He always wants the phone number of where you are so he can get in touch with you.
15. He watches out for you.
16. He doesn't like it when you go out on your own to hen parties.
17. He *listens* when you talk to him.
18. When you walk around the house with very little on, he whistles, as though you were a babe on the beach.
19. Your picture is on his desk in the office and in his wallet. He always wants to look at you.
20. When he loves you, he loves your kids.

Hopefully some or all of the above promises will motivate you to do *The Rules*. Still another incentive for doing *The Rules* is what you *won't* get:

1. No messy divorce. Instead, you have one of those made-in-heaven marriages. He'll take care of you when you're old. He really, really loves you. A *Rules* marriage is forever.

2. No outside counselling. He has no interest in couples therapy. When you do *The Rules*, he doesn't have big issues with you. He doesn't wish you were this, that or different. His love for you is unconditional. Sure, he might wish you balanced your chequebook, lost ten pounds or cleaned the house more often, but he is not seriously annoyed or upset about it. He finds it all amusing. Ultimately, he finds most things about you adorable. He doesn't feel the need to consult a professional to talk about his feelings. He's busy planning your next holiday or chasing you around the house for a quick kiss.

3. No anxiety. You're not walking on eggshells. You're not always wondering if you hurt his feelings or said the wrong thing. You know that he will always forgive you, not hurt you, that he is ready to make up with you at a moment's notice.

4. No physical abuse. When you do *The Rules*, he treats you like a fragile, delicate flower. He cups your face, rubs your back when you've had a hard day and strokes your hair as if it were silk. You don't have to worry about being battered.

5. No cheating. When you do *The Rules*, he thinks you're more beautiful than other women (even if you're not). He doesn't want to have sex with anyone but you; he can't get enough of you and even wants to build up his biceps for you. You can leave him in a room full of gorgeous women and not worry! When he loves you, he loves you!

Love Only Those Who Love You

One of the greatest payoffs of doing *The Rules* is that you grow to love only those who love you. If you have been following the suggestions in this book, you have learned to take care of yourself. You're eating well and working out. You're busy with interests and hobbies and dating, and you're not calling or chasing men. You have high self-esteem because you are not sleeping around or having affairs with married men. You love with your head, not just your heart. You are honest; you have boundaries, values and ethics. You are special, a creature unlike any other. Any man would be lucky to have you!

Because you love yourself, you are no longer interested in men who ignore you, cheat on you, hurt you either physically or emotionally, and, of course, any man who can live without you. The kind of men who once nauseated you because they were open books, called too much, wrote mushy cards and told their friends and parents about you long before you said anything to your friends and parents, you now find attractive and desirable. Of course, we don't mean to suggest that you love someone simply because he loves you. No, you love whom you love. But when a man you are interested in is crazy about you, you are happy about it. You are not bored or turned off. You don't think, 'Oh no, this is too easy.' *Love should be easy!*

As a result of doing *The Rules*, you have a new attitude. You love being loved. You think that anyone who thinks you're great is great, not a jerk. You have no desire to chase someone who hasn't noticed you, sought you out or dialled your number and asked you out. Love is finally simple and sweet, not heart-wrenching and hard.

You might be saying to yourself, 'But of course!' Yet, you'd be surprised how many of us only went after men who didn't want us. We thought it was our mission in life to reform men, make men who preferred blondes (if we are brunette) interested in us. We thought we had to work at making men love us. If love came easily, we were bored. Now we like love to be easy. We go to a dance or a party and we don't have to work at all. We just show up, do *The Rules* and whoever likes us, likes us and who doesn't, doesn't. We accept whatever happens. We're laid back and confident. We don't struggle.

You're living pain free. No more lonely Saturday nights, no more waiting for the phone to ring, no more fantasizing about the man who got away or wanted your best friend, no more jealous tantrums, no more checking his desk drawers or coat pockets for incriminating evidence. To be adored and secure at last! That's the incredible payoff you get when you do *The Rules* and you're going to love it!

Be Easy to Live With

The Rules are about playing hard to get. Once you've got him, it's about being easy to be with.

Many things can go wrong in the first few months or year of marriage. You might have fights about where you'll live. There may be money problems or family problems. You thought you wouldn't have to work so hard, that you could work part-time and start planning for kids. He says he wants you to work full-time and have kids later. He thought you would make him home-cooked meals like his mother made his father and gets angry every time you open a can of tuna.

There may be more serious problems – for example, loss of job or illness. What is *The Rule* now?

The Rule is that as hard as you worked to play hard to get is how hard you must work to be easygoing! Be kind, considerate and patient; try to overlook his faults and build up his ego – tell him how good he looks, try to see things his way. Don't expect him to see things *your* way all the time.

It's natural to want to fly off the handle every time something goes wrong in the love kingdom – we all have fantasies of marital bliss. But you must try to be serene and unselfish or you won't be a happy princess.

Let's say you've cooked him his favourite dinner, but he calls at the last minute to say he's working late and that you should eat without him. You're mad and want to scream into the phone, 'But I cooked a special meal just for you!' Instead, take a deep breath and say something like, 'You've really been working hard lately. I'm so proud of you.' Promise him a back rub when he gets home. Then get busy – read a book or clean the house. Don't tell him how disappointed you are and turn into a nag. Remember, he's working long hours for the both of you!

Or let's say it's your birthday and you know he's getting you something special but you have this thing about getting a dozen roses. So, you're on edge all day and wondering if you should give him a hint. You're also mad that you even have to say something!

So what do you do? Tell a friend, buy *yourself* flowers and forget about it. Practise being happy with what you get instead of expecting him to fulfil your every romantic fantasy. Also, give it time. The roses will come. Life is long.

In general, remember that he works hard all day – whether or not you think he does. Don't hit him with every crisis the minute he walks in the door. And remember, small acts of kindness make for a great marriage.

This isn't always easy. Sometimes you just don't feel like shaving your legs, cooking him a hot meal or being so sweet, kind and loving. Your PMS might be in high gear. How do you keep yourself going?

We think it helps to use any stress busters – yoga, meditation, aerobics, running, biking, tennis, a spa weekend and so on – to reenergize your batteries. True, it takes a lot more work to be a *Rules* wife than an ordinary one, but it's so much more rewarding in the long run, don't you agree?

You might also try reading spiritual literature, seeing a therapist or joining a support group if things get too much for you or you find yourself constantly bickering with him about little things. But whatever path you choose, remember to keep the focus on *yourself*. Don't go into therapy or exercise with the idea of changing your husband or prodding him to get healthy, too. Change *yourself* and your reaction to what he is or isn't doing.

On any given day, try to remember that an attitude of gratitude can go a long way. On bad days, try to remember the reasons you married your husband. In the middle of a fight with your husband, stop and recall all those bad blind dates, the seemingly endless search for Mr Right. That should help you not say anything too mean in the middle of a fight like, 'I wish I had never met you!' or 'I should have married someone else.' Don't dredge up the past or be mean-spirited and say things like, 'Remember the time you were late for my sister's wedding?' Tell yourself, 'I found Mr Right – how important is this?'

If you want a happy *Rules* marriage, may we suggest some more rules?

1. Don't go through his clothes, pockets and drawers looking for anything – lipstick stains, women's phone numbers, hotel receipts and such. Remember, if you're in a *Rules* marriage, he's not cheating on you. Then go about your business – read a book, exercise. Don't you have a letter to send or a drawer to clean out?

2. Don't open his mail unless it is specifically addressed to both of you. It is natural to think that what's his is yours, but that's not for you to decide. If he doesn't specifically show you something or include you in certain things, it's none of your business. Besides, the less nosy you are, the more he will want to tell you – eventually.

3. Don't hold him back from doing something he really wants to do, such as a ski weekend with a bunch of friends. He should always feel free. He should not think of you as the kind of person who wouldn't want him to be happy because it means not being with you. If you feel you have to hold him back from anything, there's a problem in the relationship. Don't try to control him. Remember, we don't make things happen or stop them from happening! We're easy to be with, we go with the flow.

4. Always try to show utter contentment with him, yourself, the world. Be carefree. You'll get less wrinkles and backaches; you'll feel less stress. He'll want you more when you're the easygoing girl he dated – a creature unlike any other. Reread *Rule 1.*

5. If you're feeling weak about *The Rules* and start acting like your old pain-in-the-neck self – angry, needy, not so nice – reread *The Rules* from the beginning. It will inspire you to act like a creature unlike any other and will remind you of the benefits of doing so. Namely, your husband will find you irresistible all over again!

6. Make time for a healthy love/sex life and spend quality time together. We know that after a hard day of work, food shopping, aerobics and so on, that you may not want to have wild sex or go to the football game with him. When you were dating you did things because you wanted to please him so that he would propose. Now that you have him, you think you don't have to try that hard.

7. Don't analyse and reanalyse your relationship or force him to talk about it. It's no secret that women like to talk about their feelings and the 'relationship' more than men do. If you feel the need to have a heart-to-heart talk with your husband, but suspect that he's not interested at that very moment, a good *Rules* credo is to wait. Talk to a friend instead. It's rarely a good conversation when he's not in the mood. Don't analyse why he doesn't want to talk. If you are relaxed and confident about your relationship, he'll be much more likely to want to discuss it with you.

   Besides, unless a talk is absolutely necessary, sometimes the best way to get your husband's attention is to look extra good and be pleasant and enthusiastic with him about your life as it currently is.

8. Don't be a nag. Don't constantly complain about the lack of money, the size of your house, what needs to be done in the house, or tell him what your friends have and what you don't have. Hopefully, you married for love, not other reasons. Remember that and don't let your relationship become adversarial. Instead of trying to make your husband feel inadequate, focus on the positive. Tell him how happy you are with him, your life and your marriage.

9. Always take the high road with friends and family. You may not get along with every one of his family members or friends. However, be careful not to criticize them in front of your husband. Realise that he knows them in a special way that you may never understand. How would you like it if he found fault with your chatty but good friends or your meddling sister? Find an impartial friend to air your grudges with. Even if you're absolutely right, try not to complain to your husband. He shouldn't think of you as a grievance collector. Collecting grievances isn't healthy, so be careful not to fall into this bad habit.

10. Try to compromise. You want to live in the city. He likes the suburbs. Your idea of a good meal is in a fancy French restaurant. He likes burgers and fries. You enjoy mushy movies, he likes horror movies with blood and gore. What to do?

Be open to new experiences. Broaden your horizons and see what you can learn from him. Maybe you'll learn to like scary movies. Failing that, remember why you married him and that being together is more important than anything in particular you do.

As hard as it may be, let him win sometimes. Why? Because your relationship is more important than always winning. Being a good sport will make you more desirable to him and he is more likely to feel that any man would be lucky to have you. He'll be more afraid of losing you because you're so wonderful to be around. He'll feel that you're easygoing, a summer breeze, not a tornado. It's a good spiritual exercise to compromise and the happiness it brings means that you always end up winning in the end.

11. Be quick to say you're sorry, preferably first. Fighting is a normal part of married life, but *Rules* women try not to yell all the time, nurse grudges, hang on to resentments or turn a minor argument into a major ordeal. When you have a fight, try not to be mean or spiteful. Don't go to bed angry and try to make up first. You'll be glad you did.

12. Be neat. This rule may sound trivial in the light of deep relationship issues, but practical ones do matter, even more than to women. Clutter, old newspapers piled around the house, stains on the carpet, runs in your stockings, dirty bathtub ... all of this is not sexy! You'll feel better when you're

organized, neat and clean, and he'll respect you more because you respect yourself. After all, what can he think of you when you don't love yourself enough to wear tights without runs or hang up your clothes?

Married women who are not naturally neat should consult those who are. Get tips on cleaning out wardrobes and filing papers or hire a cleaning lady. Cleanliness is sexy!

13. Be independent. Don't talk constantly about your fear of being alone or that you could never make it on your own. Your husband should know that you feel you are desirable, a creature unlike any other, 'a catch'. Men really want women who can live without them, but have *chosen* not to. Don't flip out (in front of him) if you hear about a couple getting divorced. Don't say, 'Oh my God. That's horrible. I just don't know what I'd do. I'd die without you!' Calmly say, 'I feel so bad for them. I hope things work out,' and then change the subject.

14. Have time out together. If you have children, make it a point to hire a baby-sitter and go out for dinner with your husband on a regular basis – without feeling guilty! Of course your children deserve your attention, but they also need to grow up with parents who have a healthy established relationship. Strive to create a sound balance, bearing in mind that time apart from them is as important as time with them.

15. Say things nicely. Nothing dampens a loving relationship like yelling or finding fault. If you are annoyed, overwhelmed or stressed, try to vent your feelings by taking a job, talking to friends or doing yoga so that you don't take it out on your husband. Even if you are frazzled, try not to pick on your husband or point out his weaknesses. For example, if you come home and he's put the baby's diaper on backward, don't make him feel bad. Say something positive like, 'Wow! It's interesting how the diaper works no matter which way it's put on.' Thank him for helping and gently show him the right way. He'll appreciate your gratitude – and he'll get it right next time!

16. Don't have exaggerated expectations. If he's working overtime or weekends or didn't get you exactly what you wanted for your birthday, don't get all bent out of shape. Ask yourself, 'How important is it?' When little problems bother you, try to be grateful that you are happily married!

True, you never have to do *The Rules* quite as hard as you did in the first three months of the relationship. But that doesn't mean that you can be selfish or inconsiderate or lazy. Remember that if you want a good marriage, *The Rules* never really end!

Rules for Girlfriends, Bosses/ Co-workers and Children

Because *The Rules* work so well with men, many women have asked us if there is a way to apply *The Rules* to platonic relationships with other people, such as girlfriends, bosses, co-workers and even children. Absolutely. *The Rules* can be applied to other people so that you have good, healthy relationships, are well-liked and not taken for granted. Here are our rules for other people:

Girlfriends

1. Do *The Rules* with men. By doing *The Rules* with men, you automatically become a good girlfriend. Think about it. You're not cancelling plans at the last minute to accept a date with a man. You take your plans with your girlfriends seriously – you don't break them for a better offer. You're loyal. Of course, you're not sleeping with, chasing or flirting with your girlfriend's boyfriend or husband. You're trustworthy.

2. Figure out who your friends are. You don't want to become a doormat. For example, if you're the one

giving all the time, calling, lending your clothes, books, money and makeup and getting little or nothing in return, pull back a little and see what happens. It's not good for you or her if the relationships is one-sided. Maybe she's not that interested in the friendship. On the other hand, if *you* are the one always taking, try to give more or not accept as much.

3. Don't be a burden. If you're going through a particularly hellish time – man, health, work issues – don't dump it all on one friend, day and night. Try to complain to several friends so that no one takes the brunt of it and you don't lose friends. Try to give back an hour for every hour they give of their time. Always remember to ask how they're doing, even if you *know* they're doing better than you. Everyone gets their fair share of good and bad in life. It all evens out in the end. To compare is to despair!

4. Be happy for your friends. If your girlfriend is getting married and you don't even have a boyfriend or she lands a great job and you hate yours, it may be hard to feel genuinely pleased by her good fortune, but you must work on summoning up these feelings. Maybe she was lucky. On the other hand, maybe she worked hard for her success – took more social actions and sent more CVs than you did. It doesn't matter. Whatever the reason, she is your friend and she deserves to feel that you are happy for her, not jealous. Rather than seethe with envy, see what you

can do about meeting a man and finding a better job of your own. Send her a congratulations card and smile at her wedding. Wishing others happiness is the best way to ensure our own.

Bosses and Co-workers

1. Don't act too casual or talk about your private life at the office. You might think talking about personal matters or your feelings at work will make you feel more at home. But your boss and co-workers will respect and trust you more if they sense that you are professional and not the gossipy type.

2. Work for the good of the company, not for your own personal gain. Every day think, 'How can I contribute to my company or help customers?' Don't think we're being corny or naive here. We know that business can be cut-throat. But when you think of the company, you automatically succeed.

3. Don't focus solely on how to get a raise or a promotion or how to do the least amount of work without getting found out. Think about doing quality work and being a good worker, or you won't feel good about yourself.

4. Don't be over-eager or volunteer to do too much too quickly in an effort to make your boss notice you. He'll find you if he needs you; be available when he does!

5. Don't be a self-centred, short-term thinker. Everyone around you will smell self-interest and think less of you.

6. Be a team player.
7. Don't work round the clock. Have a social life. Remember that work isn't everything; you will be a much better worker if you are happy in other areas of your life.

Children

Children are a lot like men. They'll take advantage of you if you let them! One of the benefits of having a *Rules* marriage is that your kids tend to treat you as nicely as your husband does. They copy his behaviour, making him their role model for how to treat you.

For example, if your son observes his father being loving and attentive and buying you cards and flowers, he will try to do the same in his own way (i.e., break his piggy bank for a bracelet or bouquet of flowers).

As we have already said, 'when he loves you, he loves your kids.' We would like to add, 'when he loves and respects you, your kids learn to love and respect you.'

In addition, here are some rules to make sure your children treat you well:

1. Don't let your children treat you as their equal. For example, if they call you by your first name, don't answer. Instead ask, 'Did you say something? I respond to the name Mum.' That way they know you're the boss.

   Similarly, don't *ask* them if they want to go to school, brush their teeth or go to bed. Tell them what they must do. Children respond well to discipline and orderliness. You are doing them a disservice when you let them run the show.

2. Don't spoil your kids. You might be tempted to overdo, particularly if you waited until later in life to have children or had to adopt to overcome infertility problems. You might want to jump every time the baby cries. Assuming the baby is fed, dry and not sick, you do not have to spend endless hours pampering him or her, or you will become trapped in a pattern that's almost impossible to break. Encourage your child to be self-sufficient. As your children get older, encourage them to help with household chores. If you let your children have some responsibility, instead of constantly doing everything for them, you will help to foster independence and competence.

3. Don't make an issue out of food. Don't force them to finish every meal; you may unknowingly begin a life of weight problems for them. Unlike adults, children eat when they're hungry and stop when they're full. They won't starve to death. Save your energy for more important matters like teaching them good manners and values.

4. Have a life! Don't feel guilty for working, talking on the phone about business or with friends. You are entitled to some time to yourself, and you'll be a better mother for having a full life. Mothers who spend too much time with or overindulge their children and neglect themselves are often frustrated

and resentful. It's not necessarily the quantity of time you spend with your child, but the quality.

In the same vein, let your child know it's not okay to interrupt you when you have company or are on the phone. Unless it's an emergency or your child is hurt or sick, tell him or her that you are busy and will talk to him or her later – and make sure you stick to your word. This way your child learns to respect your private life and learns patience. He or she will get mummy time, just later.

5. Don't buy out the toy store. You might be able to afford the best of everything, but should you buy it? We think not, unless you want your child to turn into a monster, the kind of kid who throws tantrums in a department store. So even if you can afford the whole store, restrain yourself. The same goes for pushing your child to participate in every hobby and sport. Check your motives. Are these really your child's interests or your ego at work?

6. Let your children take responsibility for their actions. If your children don't want to do their homework, try to find out why; perhaps they didn't understand the assignment. Help them, but don't do it for them. If it's just a case of being lazy or wilful, tell them they are responsible and they will have to face the consequences. If you want you can explain that you did your homework when you were growing up and that's how you got to where you are today.

7. Stick to your word. Explain to your child if he/she engages in bad behaviour – i.e., curses, hits

someone or acts out – he/she has to suffer the consequences. You decide what the punishment is – i.e., no TV – and stick to it. If you make idle threats, you will lose credibility and your children will get away with murder.

8. Encourage your child to confide in you. Lay down the law about good and bad behaviour, but always leave the door open for your child to tell you something you may not approve of. In other words, be strict, but not judgmental. That way if there's something your child doesn't want to tell you, he/she can at least tell you that much, i.e., 'I have a secret I don't want to tell you.' If you don't want to find out about your child's problems too late or from someone else, make sure your child knows that he or she can always confide in you and count on you *no matter what.*

A general tip: Good mothers are observant mothers. If you sense that your child is anxious or edgy, perhaps you want to cancel your social plans or leave work early to spend 'a kid day' or 'kid's night out', something as simple as pizza and a movie may get him or her to open up and tell you what's going on.

6 | Success Stories: Women Who Followed *The Rules* and Changed Their Lives!

Since *The Rules* came out in February 1995, thousands of women have contacted us to ask for help with this successful dating method and to share their experiences. Around the world, women are buying *The Rules* for themselves as well as for their single friends and forming support groups to help one another follow *The Rules*. Mothers are sending *The Rules* to their daughters and grandmothers are sending it to their granddaughters. The word has got out. *The Rules* work! Here are some true success stories that may inspire you to do *The Rules* better – or for the first time!

Jennifer T.'s story, Los Angeles, California

When she stopped sending a doctor greeting cards and gave him space, he decided she was 'The One'.

Jennifer T., thirty-three, called us from Los Angeles to ask for our advice. A friend sent her *The Rules* and she was anxiously trying to practise them on Mark, a thirty-one-year-old doctor, divorced for two years. She said that after four months of dating Mark, he started pulling away. She wanted to know what she was doing wrong. She was crying when she called us – she really wanted to marry this man!

We went over all the important facts – how they met, who pursued whom, what rules were broken – to pinpoint the problem.

They met on a blind date. It was instant attraction. Mark called her *early in the week* for Saturday nights for the first two months. A good sign. They started seeing each other once or twice a week. They had sex after three months. So far, so good. But one evening over dinner, Mark told her he wasn't sure how he felt and what the future would bring. What went wrong?

After some close investigation, we discovered Jennifer had strayed in several key areas. Her major slip was actually after the second date. She sent him a romantic card saying she was glad they met and signed off with, 'XO, Jennifer'. Mark didn't acknowledge the card. After spending a weekend in Aspen a month later, she sent him a second card thanking him for the trip. Again, he never called to thank her for the card.

Of course, *Rules* girls know not to send men thank-you cards. They simply thank a man in person after the date or the weekend. Putting it in writing is not necessary, shows too much interest and effort and possibly low self-esteem. He got to spend time with you! Who needs a thank-you card for that?

A romantic thank-you card tells a man exactly how you feel and destroys the mystery and challenge of pursuing you. *Rules* girls receive cards, they don't send them. Mark never sent her a card, much less said, 'I love you.'

Jennifer's other mistakes: After seeing Mark for two months, she started to accept last-minute dates on Monday nights. And when Mark told her he wasn't sure how he felt, she asked him a lot of questions to get him to pinpoint the problem. What wasn't he sure about? Was there something he didn't like that she could change? Did he still have feelings for his ex-wife?

Mark said it wasn't anything in particular. He suggested they 'take a break' for a week or two so he could sort out his feelings. Jennifer was devastated.

This is what we told her:

When a man says he's 'not sure how he feels' and wants to 'take a break' after dating you for four months, what that usually means is he feels overwhelmed by your interest and intensity. It also means that, because he knows exactly how you feel, he doesn't find you intriguing or challenging. He feels slightly bored or too comfortable, not excited about you. He may even be annoyed that you made the pursuit too easy.

We advised Jennifer not to call or write to Mark – she was thinking about sending him an 'I'm here for you when you're ready' card. We suggested that she go away with a friend on a singles holiday and take other actions to meet men, so she was busy and not waiting by the phone for Mark to call, or too eager when he did call.

We told her that if and when Mark called that she sound light and breezy and not bring up their last serious talk, but to turn him down for a date if he asked by nicely saying, 'Gosh, I'd love to, but the next couple of weeks are no good.' We suggested she end the call in ten minutes and simply say she was on her way out, if necessary.

The reason is, the only way Jennifer would ever know if Mark loved her and couldn't live without her was to let him miss her. Mark had to feel that she was slipping away and only a declaration of love could win her back. Jennifer agreed, since being with a man who was 'not sure how he felt' after four months was just too painful.

Since following this plan of action – dating others, booking a trip to Club Med, turning Mark down for a couple of dates – Jennifer called recently to report that Mark was aggressively pursuing her. For the first time, he sent her flowers and a romantic card that said, 'Miss you terribly! Love, Mark.' He asked her in advance for Saturday nights as he did when they first met. On the first date since their break-up, Mark apologized by saying, 'You know I wasn't sure how I felt before. I guess I needed some time to think. Now I know, you're the one!'

Rather than ask him to elaborate or turn that remark into a serious talk, Jennifer simply smiled. She sent him only one card since they reconciled – a simple birthday card, nothing scenic or too sweet. Three months later, Mark proposed. Jennifer is sold on *The Rules* and telling all her single friends to try them.

Barbara N.'s story, Athens, Ohio

When she stopped being 'friends' with men, she got a friend for life, a husband!

After reading *The Rules*, Barbara, a twenty-nine-year-old social worker, called us to seek advice. She confessed that her big downfall is becoming close friends with men on the rebound or men who want to talk about their girlfriends and get her advice, and then falling in love with them and getting hurt. Barbara was always caught up in some three-way relationship – waiting for a man to be dumped by the girl he really liked, or playing second fiddle to another girl. In other words, she was constantly accepting crumbs (Thursday night dates and Monday lunches). It was always the same story: These men thought Barbara was nice and sweet, but they never thought about marrying her.

When we told Barbara to stop being friends with men and to quit playing therapist to their relationship woes, she argued that she valued male friendships because she liked to know how men think to help her date better. We told her that all the dating help she needed was contained in *The Rules* and that her future husband would be her best friend. But until then, men should not be her bosom buddies.

We put Barbara on a plan of not getting into any deep conversations with men about relationships – theirs, hers or anyone else's. We knew this would be difficult. Being a social worker, Barbara loves to talk about this kind of stuff.

We also told her not to call men and rarely return their calls, and not to be so serious. This has been very hard for Barbara who feels it's 'rude' not to return calls and 'superficial' not to talk about one's feelings. But she agreed to take our advice because her way hasn't worked. She hadn't been in a satisfying relationship in five years and was tired of being alone.

Six months ago, Barbara started doing *The Rules* on Barry, whom she met at a singles bar. He approached her. After about fifteen minutes of light conversation, she forced herself to mingle (even though she would have liked to talk to him the entire night), which prompted him to ask for her phone number. She did not offer him her business card as she usually did, so he flagged down the bartender for a pen to write it down. She couldn't believe it. *The Rules* were really working!

Like clockwork, Barry called her the following Tuesday for a Saturday night date and they have been dating ever since. For the first time, Barbara is not trying to be best friends with an eligible bachelor. She doesn't accept last-minute dates to hang out in his apartment. She ends dates first. If he talks about his problems, she doesn't play therapist. She listens, she sympathizes, she's sweet, but she ends the conversation first.

Barbara used to think that a man would lose interest in her unless she solved his problems. Now she realizes that she doesn't have to be this or that or do anything really, except *The Rules*, to keep a man interested. Now she sees that a man falls in love with a woman's essence. She also didn't bring Barry into her world too soon by introducing him to family and friends before he introduced her to his.

By following *The Rules*, she let Barry simply fall in love with her – and it's working. Barry recently took Barbara as his date to his best friend's wedding. As the bride and groom walked down the aisle, he whispered, 'I want the next wedding we go to to be ours.'

Susan G.'s story, Boca Raton, Florida

After years of dating Mr Wrong, The Rules *helped this divorcee catch Mr Nice and eventually Mr Right.*

Susan, forty, a divorced interior designer, has a history of dating men who are moody, sarcastic and difficult. Her ex-husband, Brian, constantly found fault with her and her last boyfriend, Steven, withheld affection and complained that she wasn't 'there enough for him'. Susan's response was to drop her friends and hobbies to make him dinner, type his CV when he suddenly decided to change careers; she even decorated his apartment for free. The more she tried, the more he criticized. He eventually broke up with her.

Susan went to a therapist who concluded that she's attracted to men who remind her of her critical father. But after thirty sessions, Susan's therapist could not stop her from dating such men nor did she offer specific instructions on how to attract and keep desirable men.

She was just good at helping Susan see her destructive patterns.

At the suggestion of a girlfriend, Susan read *The Rules*, called us, and decided to give them a try. We advised her that in addition to following *The Rules*, she should be on the alert for men who are moody, critical, or even difficult even if she was physically attracted to them. This worked. For the first time in her life, she began to date men who treated her well, complimented her, and pursued her without much effort on her part. For the first time, she wasn't jumping through hoops to please a man, but dating with self-esteem.

Susan finally met a really considerate guy, Alan. But she wasn't sure if she liked Alan because he was nice or because she really liked him. Susan was also not sure she even wanted to get married again, but she did want a *Rules* relationship. We encouraged her to write down her feelings so she could see them in black and white and analyse them more honestly.

Susan soon realized she was not really in love with Alan, but simply forcing herself to love 'a good guy' because he was treating her well, thanks to *The Rules*! Susan concluded that she did not find Alan particularly exciting, merely kind and considerate. She was just so happy not to be mistreated that she tried to love him. Sometimes when you do *The Rules*, you don't fall in love, but you certainly don't get treated badly either!

Susan agreed with our assessment. And although it was painful to break up with 'a good guy', she did it anyway and started dating again. If you're anything like Susan, it bears repeating that *The Rules* are not about settling – that is, forcing ourselves to love a man simply because he loves us or does all the right things, like calling often and buying us flowers and so on. The purpose of *The Rules* is to get the guy you are truly crazy about to marry you.

We assured Susan that by doing *The Rules* on men she truly liked, she would get the big payoff. She would catch Mr Right. We were right. Susan has since met Robert, who she thinks is really, really sexy, not *just nice*. She thinks about him a lot and doesn't have to ask anyone if he's Mr Right. He calls her almost every day and makes her feel special.

Susan credits *The Rules* for changing her life. She feels that following *The Rules* forced her to think more highly of herself, to not accept just any treatment from a man.

Susan joined a *Rules* support group – about a dozen women who meet every week in her neighbourhood to discuss their particular dating situations and to support one another. Susan recently announced to the group that, after ten months, Robert proposed. He wanted to live together as soon as they had got engaged, but she refused, saying she was an old-fashioned girl, so he moved forward the wedding date!

Stacey G.'s story, Houston, Texas

She discovered The Rules *four years after she got married. Better late than never!*

Stacey, a thirty-three year old secretary, found out about *The Rules* a little late – four years after she got married! After reading the book, she craved a real *Rules* marriage. If anyone tells you they got married without doing *The Rules*, keep in mind that *The Rules* are not just about getting married, but having a great marriage and a husband who is attentive and really crazy about you!

Indeed, *The Rules* would have saved Stacey much heartache over the years! She met Neil, a cute stock-broker, at a health club. Both are avid exercisers. He approached her at the bicep machine, offered to show her a couple of moves, and then asked her to go for coffee after the workout.

So here we have a good *Rules* beginning – he thought she was beautiful and made the first move. But dazzled by his good looks, Stacey readily said yes and that was her first mistake. She was too eager, too available. She should have said, 'Oh, I would love to, but I can't.' Remember, we don't go for coffee on a moment's notice! This is not a game, it's because you value yourself and your time. A man has to wait to spend time with you!

That started a year's worth of last-minute dates because Neil realized he could see Stacey without giving her advance notice. Quite often, Neil would ask Stacey for a Saturday night date on a Friday afternoon. She would cancel plans with her girlfriends, only to run into Neil at the gym that Saturday afternoon and be told, 'I'm not in the mood. I think I'll hang out with the guys tonight.' She'd be crushed, but he was really cute and she thought this was the best way to 'get him'. If she wasn't always available, maybe he would think she didn't like him, or worse, ask another girl who was available! She'd cry to herself and her friends, but hoped this would lead to marriage anyway.

This went on for about two years. Neil rarely treated her well. After a romantic weekend away together – her idea – he said to her rather matter-of-factly, 'You know, Stacey, I like you, but I'm not sure I'm ever going to settle down. I like my freedom.' One Sunday afternoon she came over and offered to make dinner. He said 'great' and then left her in the kitchen while he played basketball with his friends. She cooked and cried while he shot hoops.

Not knowing what to do about this going-nowhere relationship, Stacey finally threatened to quit her well-paying job and share an apartment with her older sister in another city. She didn't know she was doing *The Rules* – she wasn't even aware of the concept. She simply had had enough and her sister suggested she give him an ultimatum: either marry me or good-bye. She took the advice. Afraid of losing her and feeling that she had been such a good sport, Neil proposed.

Four years later, Stacey wished she had some of the payoffs of a *Rules* marriage. For example, when they went to a party, Neil was always leaving her side to talk to strangers. At home, he was sometimes affectionate, but didn't try to initiate intimacy. In general, he treated her like good, old dependable Stacey – the girl who cooked while he played basketball – rather than a creature unlike any other.

We advised Stacey to study *Rule 44: Even if You're Engaged or Married, You Still Need The Rules* and apply them from this day forward. For example, we told her to wear more flattering clothes (she tends to dress conservatively), to join a gym (she stopped exercising after they got married), to leave his side and mingle when they go to parties, not to initiate intimacy or hand-holding, not to call him at work so often or leave love notes on the refrigerator door. We suggested she act a little more elusive – like the girl who threatened to leave town. After all, it was not the 'good girl' Stacey who cooked his dinner that made Neil propose, but the *Rules* part of Stacey that finally won him over.

Already Stacey has noticed a difference since applying *The Rules*. Neil calls her more often from work and is more attentive both at home and in public. He recently surprised her by taking her to a romantic inn for her thirty-third birthday. Once hopeless about changing the course of her marriage, Stacey is now a big believer in *The Rules*.

Amy D.'s story, San Diego, California

This chronic Rule-breaker learned the hard way: moving to be closer to a man makes him run the other way!

Amy, forty-three and divorced, felt she finally hit the jackpot. After seven years of being single since her husband left her and in relationships that didn't wind up at the altar, she met Jack on a business trip. Amy and Jack worked at the same computer company but in different offices – she in San Diego, he in Minneapolis. All employees were invited to corporate headquarters in Chicago to learn a new software system.

Amy noticed Jack right away and sat next to him at the seminar. Big mistake! *Rules* girls don't make things happen. A man either notices us or he doesn't, sits near us or he doesn't. Having more software experience than Jack, she offered to give him a few pointers. That's a common ploy smart women use to get a man to notice them. Unfortunately, it never works! Trying to be a gentleman, Jack took Amy out to dinner to say, 'Thank you'. One thing led to another, a few drinks, and they ended up sleeping together in his hotel room.

The fast and furious courtship continued after the seminar was over. They E-mailed and called each other constantly. He suggested she move in with him and try to get a job in the Minneapolis office. The company didn't have an opening in Minneapolis, but Amy quit her San Diego job anyway to be with Jack. (How many women have thrown away their careers and flats for a man? Of course, they always live to regret it. *Rules* girls know better!)

The first month or so of living together was pure bliss – he worked hard and she decorated and cooked while looking for work, unsuccessfully. But by the second month, the fun faded. Jack was annoyed that he was supporting Amy. He stayed at the office later and later and called at the last minute to say he wasn't coming home for dinner. On weekends, he left her alone to play golf.

Amy had no real friends in Minneapolis and became increasingly depressed and lonely. She worked up the courage to ask Jack what was going on. He told her 'things weren't working out as he expected' and to move out as soon as possible. (When you don't do *The Rules* men can be pretty cruel. They just want you gone, yesterday!)

Devastated, Amy called a friend in San Diego who offered her a couch to sleep on and a copy of *The Rules*. Amy read it in one sitting and wept, realizing all the mistakes she had made with Jack (and with other men, including her ex-husband). She spoke to Jack first and sat next to him; she used her computer smarts as an excuse to strike up a conversation; he wasn't really interested in her, just her expertise; she slept with him on the first date, which wasn't really a date, but simply his way of thanking her for computer help. And worst of all, she quit her job and left her family and friends to move in with him.

After reading *The Rules*, Amy started attending *Rules* support group meetings, practised not initiating conversations with men or helping them with business. She recently met Bruce at a computer trade show in New York City, where he lived. He approached her. After talking for fifteen minutes, Amy told him she had to get going, so he asked for her number. This was radically new behaviour for Amy, who pre-*Rules* typically told a man her whole life story right away. After the show, Bruce called her, made a special trip to San Diego to visit her, and sent her postcards in between visits for the first few months. After dating for eight months, he proposed and said he would move to San Diego.

Amy just can't believe it. This is the first time she didn't have to make things happen with a man, the first time she let a man do all the work ... and it worked! They're planning a June wedding and she's keeping her flat and her job. For a savvy business woman who first thought *The Rules* were for 'other women' Amy is now leading a *Rules* support group and loving it!

Do you have a *Rules* story? We would love to hear how you are using *The Rules* to get engaged or married or date successfully. Please write to us at:

The Rules
FDR Station,
P.O. Box 6047
New York, N.Y. 10150
U.S.A.

7 | Answers to Frequently Asked Questions About *The Rules*

Q: If I do *The Rules*, how will he know the real me?

A: On dates you *are* yourself. There's a big difference between being mysterious and being deceptive. You don't lie, you just don't open up too fast. You don't bring up subjects that would tip your hand, such as marriage, the future, children, or feel you have to answer questions that would reveal too much too soon or make you uncomfortable.

For example, if he asks why 'a nice girl like you is not married,' you can casually say, 'I really haven't thought about it' and then change the subject. Don't say anything depressing like, 'I haven't been on a date in six years' or 'It's really hard to meet men.' Don't say anything cynical like, 'I guess I'm just lucky.'

The point is, you don't have to answer every question he asks you. Your dating history is none of his business on the first, second or third dates. Realize that if he really presses the issue, he probably is either not that nice, or not that interested in you. When a man is interested in you, he doesn't want to make you uncomfortable.

Don't worry, 'the real you' will definitely shine through. Your conversation, your appearance, your laugh – all of these are uniquely yours and will help him to discover the creature unlike any other that is you.

Q: If I do *The Rules* how will he know I like him?

A: You say 'yes' when he asks you out by Wednesday for Saturday night. You show up on the date – you smile, you're warm and pleasant, fun to be with, you thank him for a nice evening. That's how he knows you like him.

Contrary to popular belief, you do not have to call men or send them thank-you notes or buy them presents for them to see that you are interested.

If you like him, but he calls too late in the week for you to accept the date, you say, 'I'd love to, but I have plans.' By saying 'I'd love to,' and declining nicely, with genuine regret, he'll know you would actually like to spend time with him, you're just busy. If he likes you, he'll call again. But next time it will be earlier in the week.

Q: What do I do when a man gives me his business card and says 'Call me?'

A: Look at the card as if no man has even given you one before, smile and sweetly say, 'No thanks, I don't think so.'

Rules girls don't call men and have no use for their business cards or phone numbers. If a man is really interested in you, he will then ask for your number. Don't say, 'I don't call men. It's better if you call me.' That's telling him what to do. He either asks for your number on his own or he doesn't. You only want men who *want* your number.

Q: What if a man leaves a message on your answering machine on Wednesday? Can you call him back to secure a weekend date?

A: In the first month of dating, it's best not to call him back at all. This way he'll have to call again (at the beginning of the following week) if he really wants to see you. Better to lose one Saturday night date than show too much interest and risk destroying a potentially long-term relationship.

The first month should establish a pattern: he is the hunter – calling you and calling you, if only to just find you in! Better that he keep trying to pin you down and not actually reach you in time for a Saturday night date than your calling him back right away and being readily available. By not calling back, some women we know didn't actually have dates with men for a month or so, but now they're married to them. They set the chase in motion and created longing.

Of course, if he calls you two or three times in one week and still gets your machine, a quick call back can be okay. Use your common sense. Remember, we said you should *rarely* return his calls, not *never!*

After the first month, you can return his calls a day or two later or call him occasionally (say, once for every four of his calls), preferably when he's not home. If he absolutely insists you call him, call once in a while so that he doesn't think you're not interested.

Q: If a friend sets you up on a blind date and the date goes very well, do you call the friend to thank her and to tell her you like him?

A: No, don't call the friend to thank her or express interest in the person she introduced you to. This may sound harsh or rude, but *The Rules* answer is to make a mental note to do something nice for the friend in the future. To call and tell is to kiss and tell. She'll either inadvertently mention to him that you called or possibly call him to tell him so, and he'll definitely interpret it as a sign of interest in him. Let *him* call her to find out what you thought of him. If your friend does ask, you should keep your answer as evasive as possible. For example, you can say, 'He seemed nice! We had fun.' This is noncommittal but positive – just the tone you want to take.

Q: Do *The Rules* work on all men?

A: Fortunately, yes. *The Rules* work on all men from all countries and from all walks of life. And that's actually a good thing. It means we don't have to rewrite *The Rules* for every nationality, or every time we meet a man or figure out how the man we're dating is the exception to *The Rules*.

We do not have to initiate relationships with 'shy men' and only play hard to get with corporate titans. We believe all men like a challenge and that men are not shy when they see a woman they are attracted to. If they don't make the first move, it's because there may be no spark and they are simply not that interested! The same man you think is shy will jump on a plane to be with the woman he's crazy about. The same man you've chased for five years and called 'commitment-phobic' will marry another girl in six months.

Women try to tell us otherwise. We've been told some men are withdrawn and that's why women have to approach them. We've been told some men are talkative, so how can one get off the phone in ten minutes? We've been told some men need women to mother them because they didn't get enough attention or nurturing as children. Yet these men do not necessarily marry their 'nurturing' girlfriends, but the women who were slightly aloof, laughed and didn't play saviour, the girls who didn't care too much too soon.

That's why you should do *The Rules* even if you meet a man in a relationship workshop or a programme where feelings are freely discussed and defences are down. A man is still a man and still likes a challenge *even* if he attends weekend seminars on self-improvement or goes to Tibet for spiritual healing. That means that even if he 'opens up too fast' and talks about his feelings right away, you should still be 'honest but mysterious'. *The Rules* supersede any philosophy, therapy, or religion he may be involved in because he's a man before he's anything else!

So rather than trying to figure out every man's ethnicity, character, or upbringing, simply do The Rules on every man you meet. You will have plenty of time down the road to be his salt of the earth, his Rock of Gibraltar, and his soul mate when you're married!

Q: My problem is not *The Rules*, but finding men to do them on. Any suggestions?

A: *The Rules* is not a guide to finding eligible men, but how to behave once you've met them. But since so many women have asked for help in meeting men, we'd like to offer some suggestions.

Two thoughts to get you going: Your chances of meeting a man greatly improve when you leave your house, so get off the couch! And remember, you only have to find one!

Also keep in mind that you shouldn't go out blindly, but try to go to places that singles frequent, not married couples and/or kids.

So why don't you try?

1. Club Med or any singles holiday.
2. Church or synagogue or other place of worship.
3. Jogging in the park.

4. Joining a gym.
5. Taking up a male-dominated sport such as golf, scuba diving, tennis or skiing.
6. Putting a personal ad in a newspaper or magazine.
7. Signing up with a dating service.
8. Joining a ski house.
9. Meeting friends for dinner at a trendy restaurant (where men hang out at the bar).
10. Going to a lecture or book signing that would draw men.
11. Taking a summer share in a house.
12. Asking friends to fix you up (but don't be too aggressive about it!).

However, wherever you go, whatever you do, don't talk to any man first, *sit or stand next to him* hoping he'll notice you.

Q: If I can't talk about my feelings or my past relationships on dates, what can I talk about?

A: Sports, politics, your favourite books and movies, museums, the Internet, work, weather and dining (the restaurant, the meal, the ambiance). Dating is not a therapy session – talk about subjects outside yourself. There's a whole world out there!

Q: The book is so popular, what if a man asks you point blank, 'Are you doing *The Rules* on me? Is that why you don't call me?'

A: You could say, '*What rules?*' and hope he thinks you've never heard of the book and drops the subject. Also remember, just because a man asks a question doesn't mean you have to answer it. But if you feel compelled to say something, you can say, 'Actually, I'm just not a big caller.' Before reading *The Rules*, you called men more often, now you don't. We've all read advice books that have deeply influenced us and incorporated some of their ideas into our lives until it became who we are. Now it's part of your personality to rarely call men! (Besides, no one can prove you're doing *The Rules*!)

Q: How do I know if he's 'The One'?

A: If you are feeling ambivalent, we suggest you ask yourself these questions: 'Do I like to kiss him? Can I wake up with him for the rest of my life? Do I like his voice, talking to him, the way he dances, the way he treats people? Do I like the way he treats me? Do I like him as a person?' The answers to these questions really matter on a day-to-day basis. *You have to really like just being with him!*

Of course, we cannot tell you how to feel about a man, but it's best if you feel something like, 'Wow, I've got to marry this man! I must be with him.' If you are tortured, confused or have to make a list of his pros and cons, it's not a good sign. If you're forcing yourself to like him because he *appears* to be the proper match (your mother loves him, your friends say he's perfect for you, and he makes a good living) but he's not your type, you may be settling. Trust your gut feelings!

Q: I went out with a man who at the end of the date said he had a great time and would call again. He never called. Why? It's been a month. I thought I did *The Rules*. May I call him to find out what went wrong?

A: Don't be surprised. We hear from many women who have this happen to them. Some men are just being polite when they say it. Some had a good time, but didn't really want to go out with you again. A *Rules* girl doesn't spend a whole lot of time trying to figure it out. She moves on ...

We don't recommend calling him for an explanation. It's simply not *The Rules* to chase a man or put him on the spot. And what could he possibly say without hurting your feelings? But if you absolutely must call, wait a considerable amount of time until you're sure he's not going to call you, then go ahead. Better to break *The Rules* with this (dead) man than with a real candidate.

Q: How can I meet his parents and friends before he meets mine if he moved from L.A. to New York and everyone he knows is on the West Coast?

A: Hold off for as long as possible from introducing him to your family and friends before you meet his. If he's truly in love, he'll probably tell his parents about you and they may book a trip to New York to meet you. Or, since he's living in New York he has probably established his own 'New York family' – close friends, his boss, co-workers – so at least wait until after he introduces you to them.

Q: You have a date for Saturday night, but it's Saturday afternoon and he still hasn't called to confirm. Do you call him and ask, 'What's up? Do we still have plans?'

A: No, you act as if you knew you had a date, and be dressed and ready to go when he does call or shows up at your door. In other words, he should never know that you wondered all day (and possibly all week!) if you'd ever hear from him again. If he doesn't call and forgot the date, don't call him. Just know that one day he could forget your wedding date. *Next!*

Q: At a party, is it okay to make eye contact or smile at a man?

A: You can look at him if he looks at you. By all means, smile back if he smiles at you. You just don't initiate anything, from flirting to standing in front of him to make him notice you. On the other hand, you don't have to look down to avoid his gaze if he stares at you, or turn your back to him. You're polite, you just don't pursue men!

Q: I don't like to give out my home number to a man I just met. Is it okay to take his number and call him?

A: While we understand the safety reasons for not giving a stranger your home number, we're not fond of this approach. It throws off *The Rules*. How do you know he was really going to call you? Sometimes a man doesn't know how to say, 'It was nice meeting you. Have a nice life.' Instead, out of politeness, he says, 'Can I have your number? Maybe we can get together sometime.' You say, 'Well, actually, I don't give out my number. Why don't you give me yours?' You call him and feel justified in doing so. After all, he did *ask* for your number. And then you wonder why the relationship doesn't work out.

We suggest you try to figure out a way for men to get in touch with you first – whether it's by giving them your work number or getting a personal voice-mail number – so that they can make the first move. That way you keep your privacy, but you can still do *The Rules*. Of course, if there is no other way, try to wait a week before you call him. But keep in mind, even if you call him, he must still be the one to ask you out. If he hasn't done so within ten minutes, end the conversation and move on. If you do go on a date, and after spending several hours with him you still feel uncomfortable giving him your number, you probably have reservations about him and might want to move on to someone you do feel comfortable giving your number to.

8 | Last But Not Least – 32 Extra Hints

1. When he asks you out, silently count to five before saying yes. It will make him nervous and that's good!
2. Don't call him even when you feel mean about not calling him. If he loves you, he'll call anyway. When he asks you to call him, call him once. Do the absolute minimum!
3. When he asks you out for ice cream, a drink or to a football game when you wish you were going out for a fancy dinner, say 'Sure!' Remember, you're hard to get but easy to be with! You'll go to an expensive restaurant another time.
4. When walking down the street, drop *his* hand first, ever so slightly.
5. *The Rules* are written in stone, but how you do them will depend on your temperament. If you're an overly nice, gushy girl, do *The Rules* like boot camp. The stricter, the better, that is never call him or return his phone calls very infrequently. But if you're already cool or aloof by nature, be extra

sweet when you do *The Rules*. Call him once for every five times he calls you. Be affectionate. As long as you're not asking him out or moving in or bringing up marriage, you can show him you like him a little more on each date.

6. If he's being a bad boy, taking you for granted or you want to shake things up to make him propose faster, book a trip for a week. If things are going well but you still want to a make him miss you, plan a weekend away with a girlfriend. Tell him a week before you go, in a very innocent, sweet voice, that you're going to Barcelona with your girlfriend to get a tan and relax. 'Nothing serious, just some R & R.'

7. If you are unsure about him, double date with a *Rules*-minded friend. She will tell you whether he's planning to marry you or not.

8. Even men who are in love with you and want to marry you will occasionally say things to irk you or make you nervous, such as, 'I'll take you there if we're still seeing each other next year ... you know how relationships go.' Don't get paranoid, just ignore him. Most girls would make a big fuss about it and get mad. *Rules* girls stay calm when men tease them.

9. Don't let them know you're *afraid* to be alone, to be without a man. Women who let men know how much they *need* to be with someone invite bad behaviour. Then he knows you'll put up with anything not to be alone.

10. Don't get angry if he's taking longer than you'd like to propose. Most women want to be proposed to *yesterday*. Whatever you do, don't blow up at him and press the issue. You've waited this long, hang in there. If you're doing *The Rules*, it will happen!

11. Don't get sloppy about your looks. Continue to exercise. Men don't leave women who put on twenty pounds after the wedding or the first baby, but if you want your fiancé or husband to keep drooling over you, keep fit.

12. Read the newspaper and books so you can talk to your life partner about things other than your work issues or dirty nappies. Men want wives who can fulfil them mentally as well as physically and emotionally.

13. You just found out about *The Rules* but you're already in a relationship. What can you do? Start doing *The Rules* today! Yes, you can do *The Rules* midstream. Starting right now, don't call him, don't beep him, and don't stay on the phone for more than ten minutes when he calls you. If you are seeing him every night, see him only once or twice a week. If he asks why, you're busy, busy, busy! If he asked you to go away for a week, tell him you can only go away for a three-day weekend – your job is hectic, that kind of thing. If you're living with him but you don't have an engagement ring or a wedding date, start looking in the real-estate section of the newspaper for a flat. Get the idea? Whatever you're doing, cut back. If you're giving

too much or losing yourself, pull away and see what happens!

14. On dates or in phone conversations, don't use the words 'nurturing', 'relationships', 'bonding' or talk about getting your needs met. You don't want to sound like a walking relationship book. In the early stages of dating, staying light is essential.

15. Make sure whatever message you record on your answering machine is sensible and in good taste, not outlandish. In the course of returning hundreds of women's phone calls, we have heard pretty crazy stuff – everything from wild cowboy music to the lyrics of very sensual songs to special holiday greetings. Outrageous messages show that you are trying too hard and that can easily alarm or turn off some men. You don't have to express your creativity on your answering machine. Err on the conservative side. A pleasant message is usually the best, something like: 'Hi, You've reached Karen. I can't come to the phone right now. Please leave a message.'

16. Don't be jealous if your boyfriend's or husband's ex-girlfriend calls him or sends him letters. As long as *he's* not initiating the calls and letters, you have nothing to worry about. No one can take away what's yours.

17. If you're on the phone and he calls on the other line, do not get off the phone every time for him. You don't want to seem too interested or the kind of woman that will cut short an important call with a friend or business associate the second a man calls.

Just tell him, 'Oh, I'm on the other line. Can you call me back in ten minutes [or whatever time is convenient for you]?' That way you don't have to call him and he calls you again, but make sure to be available when he calls back.

18. Don't send a man letters, brochures or news-paper/magazine clippings that you think they'd be interested in. Tell a friend that you were going to send them these items and then throw them away. Men can find this kind of attention too intense. Sometimes they don't even acknowledge it or bother to thank you. You might think they're rude or didn't receive the material. The real reason is you overwhelmed them!

19. If you think a man is doing *The Rules* on you because he's pulling back, ending the calls and dates first – he probably isn't. He may just not be that crazy about you. When a man loves you, he just wants to be with you. If he doesn't seem to be pursuing you, he probably isn't really interested.

20. If you are doing *The Rules*, but aren't getting any dates, the problem may not be *The Rules*. (In other words, don't use this as an excuse to ask men out.) You must either go out more often – try personal ads and dating services – or consider improving your appearance, if necessary. Try wearing contact lenses instead of glasses, try working out more or eating less if you're not in great shape or updating your wardrobe. Keep working on yourself, look your best and then men will come!

21. Now that *The Rules* is a best-seller, a man might have heard of it and think you are doing *The Rules* on him. Not to worry. Even if he does suspect you're doing *The Rules*, it won't reverse its effectiveness.

22. How to compete with all the *Rules* girls out there? You don't, except to keep doing *The Rules*. When a man likes you, he likes *you*.

23. Remember to say 'please' and 'thank you' on dates as well as to friends, family members and business associates. *Rules* girls are a refreshing breed — they're polite! They value themselves and the people they come in contact with.

24. The first or second date can be a Thursday or any week night. But the third date *should* be a Saturday night.

25. Remember, if he's attracted to you and you're quiet on the date, he thinks you're not a big talker. If you're not his type, he thinks you're boring. This just goes to show you, you don't have to try too hard.

26. If he's dating others, you should date others as well. We're not exclusive until he wants to be exclusive and he brings it up.

27. Try not to speak to him every day. If you're following *The Rules*, you're seeing him once or twice a week for the first month or two. But what if he's *calling* every day or several times a day, just to chat? What if he beeps you every day? Should you speak to him every time? No, you shouldn't be that accessible. Leave

your answering machine on at home sometimes and say it's hard to talk at work. You don't have to return his beeps – let him get into the habit of beeping you to let you know he's thinking about you without necessarily getting a response. You should be busy and mysterious. If you've been talking daily, talk every other day (when he calls). The rest of the time, he should get your machine. Let him miss you. If he wants to talk to you several times a day, let him marry you!

28. Don't tell men you're doing *The Rules*. Do not explain or discuss *The Rules* with men and don't tell them how to date. We've heard stories of women who actually tell men, 'You have to call me by Wednesday if you want to see me Saturday.' That's not *The Rules*. That's revealing your hand; it's like wearing a slip without a dress. *The Rules* answer is to tell a man who calls late in the week, 'Thanks, but I have plans.' He must figure out that if he wants to see you on Saturday, he'll have to call you earlier in the week. We can't make a man really interested in us by telling him when to call. He either is or isn't. You'll find out fast by doing *The Rules*.

29. Don't go away with a man for a week. Save it for your honeymoon! What if, after dating Mr Right for a month or two, he invites you on a cruise or to an exotic island for a week? *The Rules* answer? You're busy and can't get away. Cruises and week-long holidays make men go backward! Things can get hot and heavy when you see each other seven

days a week, twenty-four hours a day. You might act too wifey – telling him to watch his fat intake or giving him advice about a family or business problem. He might be romantic on the trip, but pull back when you return, saying he needs his 'space'. You may not hear from him for a week or two. The only big trip you should take is your honeymoon. He can take you for an overnight or weekend trip occasionally after dating you for three or four months, but that's it!

30. How to end a relationship or stop seeing someone you like but aren't crazy about? As soon as you're sure he's not for you, just say, 'I think you're great, but I just don't feel a spark' or 'I don't think this is working out for me.' It's not good for you to tie yourself up with someone you don't love – and it's not good for him either. If he really cares about you, you could end up leading him on and preventing him from meeting someone else. That's not fair. Remember, following *The Rules* saves you both a lot of heartache.

31. Don't have more than one drink on dates so that you do *The Rules*, end the dates first and, most important, remember what happened!

32. Remember, Cinderella ended the date first!